KON-TIKI

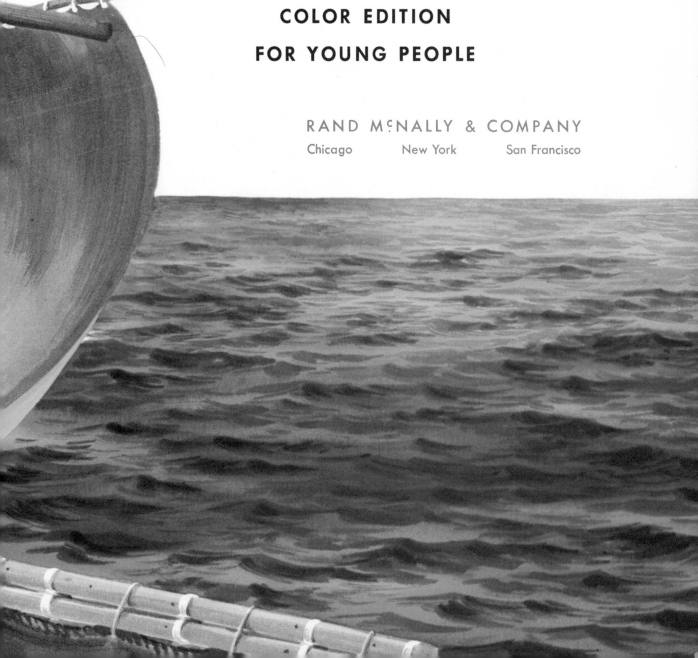

KON-TIKI

by Thor Heyerdahl

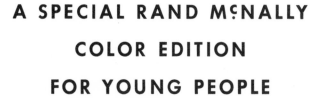

**A SPECIAL RAND McNALLY
COLOR EDITION
FOR YOUNG PEOPLE**

RAND McNALLY & COMPANY

Chicago   New York   San Francisco

About the Illustrations

The color illustrations for this new edition of KON-TIKI, including the jacket and front end-paper, were painted by William Neebe. Most of these color illustrations were based on actual photographs.

Many new photographs for use in the book were supplied through the kind cooperation of the Kon-Tiki Museum in Oslo, Norway, where the original *Kon-Tiki* raft is now preserved. Major Knut Haugland, one of the members of the Kon-Tiki Expedition, is now director of the Museum. Special acknowledgment is made to the Museum for permission to use the copyrighted diagram of the raft on p. 42.

Acknowledgment is also made to Mr. Roman Vishniac for permission to use his photograph of forms of plankton as the basis for the illustration on p. 76.

The illustrations on pp. 97 and 98 are from AKU-AKU: The Secret of Easter Island, copyrighted 1958 by Thor Heyerdahl.

The illustrations on pp. 18, 43, and 91 are adapted from old engravings and prints as reproduced in AMERICAN INDIANS IN THE PACIFIC, by Thor Heyerdahl, copyright under the Berne Convention, 1952. The drawing on p. 15 is adapted from Bennett, W. C. "Excavations in Tiahuanaco." Anthrop. Papers Amer. Mus. Nat. Hist. Vol. 34.

Copyright © 1960 by Thor Heyerdahl

Copyright 1960 under International Copyright Union by Thor Heyerdahl

Adapted from KON-TIKI: Across the Pacific by Raft, Copyright 1950 by Thor Heyerdahl

Library of Congress Catalog Card No. 60-14279
Printed in U.S.A.

First printing, 1960
Second printing, 1964
Third printing, 1966

First paperback printing, 1975

Contents

Between the little island of Fatu Hiva and the coast of South America rolls 4,000 unbroken miles of the Pacific Ocean.

1. *How It All Began*

The Marquesas Islands are a part of Polynesia and are volcanic in origin.

ONCE IN A WHILE you find yourself in an odd situation. You get into it by degrees and in the most natural way but, when you are right in the midst of it, you are suddenly astonished and ask yourself how in the world it all came about.

If, for example, you put out to sea on a wooden raft with a parrot and five companions, it is certain that sooner or later you will wake up one morning out at sea and begin to think about it.

On one such morning I sat writing in a dew-drenched logbook:

May 17. Norwegian Independence Day. Heavy sea. Fair wind. I am cook today and found several flying fish on deck, one squid on the cabin roof, and one unknown fish in Torstein's sleeping bag. . . .

Here the pencil stopped, and the same thought interjected itself: This is really a queer seventeenth of May—indeed, taken all around, a most peculiar existence. How did it all begin?

Perhaps the whole thing started the winter before, in the office of a New York museum. But it is more likely that it began ten years earlier, on a little island in the middle of the Pacific Ocean. The island was called Fatu Hiva and it was one of the islands in the Marquesas group.

I could see that little island clearly, with its jagged rust-red mountains, the green jungle that flowed down their slopes toward the sea, and the slender palms that waited and waved along the shore.

I saw the narrow Ouia Valley, where it opened out toward the sea, and remembered so well how my wife and I sat there on the lonely beach and looked out over this same endless sea, evening after evening. We were collecting all sorts of creatures and things of the present and of the past.

I remembered very well one particular evening. We had lived on the island for nearly a year, the only white people there. We lived in a hut we had built for ourselves, on piles under the palms down by the shore, and ate what the tropical woods and the Pacific had to offer us.

On that particular evening we sat, as so often before, down on the beach in the moonlight, with the sea in front of us. We filled our nostrils with an aroma of rank jungle and salt sea and heard the wind's rustle in leaves and palm tops. At regular intervals all other noises were drowned by the great breakers that rolled straight in from the sea and rushed in foaming over the land till they were broken up into circles of froth among the shore boulders. There was a roaring and rustling and rumbling among millions of glistening stones, till all grew quiet again when the sea water had withdrawn to gather strength for a new attack on the invincible coast.

"It's queer," said my wife, "but there are never breakers like this on the other side of the island."

"No," said I, "but this is the windward side; there's always a sea running on this side."

We kept on sitting there and admiring the sea as it came rolling in from eastward, eastward, eastward.

So had the ocean swells and the lofty clouds above them rolled up over the same eastern horizon since the morning of time. The first natives who reached these islands knew well enough that this was so, and so did the present islanders. The long-range ocean birds kept to the eastward on their daily fishing trips to be able to return with the eastern wind at night when the belly was full and the wings tired. Even trees and flowers were wholly dependent on the rain produced by the eastern winds, and all the vegetation grew accordingly. And we knew by ourselves, as we sat there, that far, far below that eastern horizon, where the clouds came up, lay the open coast of South America. There was nothing but 4,000 miles of open sea between.

THE OLD MAN OF THE ISLAND

We gazed at the driving clouds and the heaving moonlit sea, and we listened to an old man who squatted half-naked before us and stared down into the dying glow from a little smoldering fire.

"Tiki," the old man said quietly, "he was both god and chief. It was Tiki who brought my ancestors to these islands where we live now. Before that we lived in a big country beyond the sea."

He poked the coals with a stick to keep them from going out. Tei Tetua, the old man, sat thinking. He lived in the past. He worshiped his forefathers and their deeds in an unbroken line back to the time of the gods. And he looked forward to being reunited with them. Old Tei Tetua was the sole survivor of all the extinct tribes on the east coast of Fatu Hiva. How old he was he did not know, but his wrinkled, bark-brown, leathery skin looked as if it had been dried in sun and wind for a hundred years. He was one of the few on these islands that still remembered and still believed in his father's and his grandfather's legendary stories of the great Polynesian chief-god Tiki, son of the sun.

When we crept to bed that night in our little pile hut, old Tei Tetua's stories of Tiki and the islanders' old home beyond the sea continued to haunt my brain, accompanied by the muffled roar of the surf in the distance. It sounded like a voice from far-off times, which, it seemed, had something it wanted to tell, out there in the night. I could not sleep. It was as though time no longer existed, and Tiki and

Old Tei Tetua was one of the few natives of Fatu Hiva who remembered and believed the ancient legends of the chief-god Tiki.

Stone statues in honor of the god Tiki are found on many islands in Polynesia, including Fatu Hiva. They are very similar to statues found in South America.

Tiki, the ancestor god of the Polynesians, might have landed on a small mountainous island such as this after drifting across the Pacific.

his seafarers were just landing in the surf on the beach below. A thought suddenly struck me and I said to my wife: "Have you noticed that the huge stone figures of Tiki in the jungle are very much like the ones left by extinct civilizations in South America?"

I felt sure that a roar of agreement came from the breakers. And then they slowly subsided while I slept.

A MYSTERIOUS RACE

In the years that followed, breakers and jungle ruins were a kind of unreal dream which formed the background to my studies of the Pacific peoples. The Pacific islands were unknown to our own race until after the time of Columbus, when European caravels for the first time sailed westwards into the Pacific, with the trade wind from South America at their backs. Since then, investigators in all branches of science have collected an almost bottomless store of information about the native people who had already settled these far-flung islands before the European sailing ships arrived. But there has never been any agreement as to their mysterious origin, or the reason why the people living on all the islands

The triangular area on this map is the region known as Polynesia. According to ancient traditions, these islands were first settled by a race of white-skinned people with red hair.

nearest America were different from those next to Australia and Asia.

When the first European sailors at last ventured to enter this greatest of all oceans, they discovered to their amazement that right out in the midst of it lay a number of small mountainous islands and flat coral reefs, isolated from each other and from the world in general by vast areas of sea. And every single one of these islands was already inhabited by people who had come there before them—tall, handsome people who met them on the beach with dogs and pigs and fowl. Where had they come from? They talked a language which no other tribe knew. And the men of our race, who boldly called themselves the discoverers of the islands, found cultivated fields and villages with temples and huts on every single habitable island. On some islands, indeed, they found old pyramids, paved roads, and carven stone statues as high as a four-story house. But the explanation of the whole mystery was lacking. Who were these people, and where had they come from?

The larger islands in the west Pacific lay closely packed and were surely peopled by migrants from Asia who met little or no obstacles on their eastward move. Negroid tribes with black skin and frizzy hair went farther than the rest and stopped only in the Melanesian groups, where the wide-open span of ocean begins. Farther east the enormous unsheltered Pacific stretches directly to the South American shores, dotted only here and there by tiny and lonely island specks which are known jointly as Polynesia, the home of the Polynesian tribes.

Modern scientific research tells us that there have been no sunken land bridges in the Polynesian part of the Pacific as long as mankind has existed. Accordingly, the first inhabitants of these islands must at some time, willingly or unwillingly, have come drifting or sailing to these remote islands. Modern science has also shown that at least two different races of man have mixed to form the present Polynesian people, and that the Polynesian islands actually have been reached by two distinct waves of migration. The last to arrive, although racially unlike the Malay people, speak a language related to theirs. They probably followed the Philippine and Japan Currents across the far North Pacific, and reached Hawaii from the northwest American coast, where racial and cultural traces give evidence of early contact.

But these migrants through the North Pacific were not the real discoverers of Polynesia. Wherever they spread, from Hawaii in the north to New Zealand in the south, from Samoa in the west to Easter Island in the east —an area of open sea four times the size of all of Europe—they met an earlier people of another race. Polynesian traditions throughout the islands insist that these were a white people with red hair who spoke another language. They were far advanced in knowledge and culture, as can be verified by their large statues and stone constructions which are still left in our day, to the marvel of modern engineers.

THE LEGEND OF KON-TIKI

Even when the Europeans came to the Polynesian islands, they were quite astonished to find that many of the natives had almost white skins, fine and wavy hair varying from reddish to blonde, blue-grey eyes, and strongly hooked noses. In contrast, the genuine Polynesians had golden-brown skins, black, coarse hair, and rather flat, pulpy noses. The red-haired individuals were called *urukehu*, and were said to descend directly from the first chiefs on the islands, who were now considered gods, such as Tangaroa, Kane, and Tiki. It was Tiki, the legendary son of the sun, who had led the people to these islands, according to the story of the old native. It was his statues

that looked so much like the statues left behind by an unknown culture in early South America.

I continued to search. And I found what I hoped for. I was sitting reading the Inca legends of the sun-king Virakocha, who was the supreme head of the mythical white people in Peru. I read:

.... Virakocha is an Inca (Ketchua) name and consequently of fairly recent date. The original name of the sun-god Virakocha, which seems to have been more used in Peru in old times, was Kon-Tiki or Illa-Tiki, which means Sun-Tiki or Fire-Tiki. Kon-Tiki was high priest and sun-king of the Incas' legendary 'white men' who had left the enormous ruins on the shores of Lake Titicaca. The legend runs that the mysterious white men with beards were attacked by a chief named Cari who came from the Coquimbo Valley. In a battle on an island in Lake Titicaca the fair race was massacred, but Kon-Tiki himself and his closest companions escaped and later came down to the Pacific coast, whence they finally disappeared oversea to the westward. ...

*   *   *

Then, in 1940, the Nazi army burst into Norway and my work was interrupted. Right face, left face, about face. Washing barracks stairs, polishing boots, radio school, parachute —and at last a Murmansk convoy to the Arctic battlefield of Finnmark.

Peace came. And one day my theory was complete. I must go to America and put it forward.

Two drawings of a statute of the sun-god Virakocha, or Kon-Tiki, found in Peru. The larger drawing on the right shows more clearly the typical curled-up beard and the lightning rays around the forehead.

15

2. An Expedition Is Born

So IT HAD BEGUN, by a fire on a South Sea island, where an old native sat telling legends and stories of his tribe. Many years later I sat with another old man, this time in a dark office on one of the upper floors of a big museum in New York.

Round us, in well-arranged glass cases, lay pottery fragments from the past. The walls were lined with books. Some of them one man had written and hardly ten men had read. The old man, who had read all these books and written some of them, sat behind his work-table, white-haired and good-humored. But now, for sure, I had trodden on his toes, for he gripped the arms of his chair uneasily and looked as if I had interrupted him in a game of solitaire.

"No!" he said. "Never!"

I imagine that Santa Claus would have looked as he did then if someone had dared to affirm that next year Christmas would be on Midsummer Day.

"You're wrong, absolutely wrong," he said, and shook his head indignantly to drive out the idea.

"But you haven't read my arguments yet," I urged, nodding hopefully toward the manuscript which lay on the table.

He pushed the unopened manuscript carefully to one side and leaned over the table.

"It's quite true that South America was the home of some of the most curious civilizations of the past, and that we know neither who they were nor where they vanished when the Incas came into power. But one thing we do know for certain—that none of the peoples of South America got over to the islands in the Pacific."

He looked at me searchingly and continued: "Do you know why? The answer's simple enough. They couldn't get there. They had no boats!"

Attempts to interest scientific authorities in the "Kon-Tiki" theory proved unsuccessful.

"They had rafts," I objected hesitatingly. "You know, balsa-wood rafts."

The old man smiled and said calmly:

"Well, you can try a trip from Peru to the Pacific islands on a balsa-wood raft."

I could find nothing to say. It was getting late. We both rose. The old scientist patted me kindly on the shoulder as he saw me out, and said that if I wanted help I had only to come to him.

That evening I went down and knocked on the door of an old house in an out-of-the-way corner of Greenwich Village. I liked bringing my little problems down here when I felt they had made life a bit tangled.

A sparse little man with a long nose opened the door a crack before he threw it wide open with a broad smile and pulled me in. He took me straight into the little kitchen, where he set me to work carrying plates and forks while he himself doubled the quantity of the savory-smelling concoction he was heating.

"Nice of you to come," he said. "How goes it?"

"Rottenly," I replied. "No one will read the manuscript."

He filled the plates and we attacked the contents.

"But what did your old friend at the museum say today?"

"He wasn't interested, either," I muttered. "He said that, as long as the Indians had only open rafts, it was foolish to consider that they might have discovered the Pacific islands."

The little man thought a long time.

"Yes," he said at last. "To tell the truth, to me too that seems a practical objection to your theory."

I looked gloomily at the little ethnologist whom I had thought to be a sworn ally.

"Carl," I said. "I'm so sure the Indians crossed the Pacific on their rafts that I'm willing to build a raft of the same kind myself and cross the sea just to prove that it's possible."

"You're mad!" My friend took it for a joke and laughed, half-scared at the thought. "You're mad! A raft?"

He did not know what to say and only stared at me with a queer expression, as though waiting for a smile to show that I *was* joking.

He did not get one. I saw now that in practice no one would accept my theory because of the apparently endless stretch of sea between Peru and Polynesia, which I was trying to bridge with no other aid than a prehistoric raft.

AT THE SAILORS' HOME

My rent became due that week. At the same time a letter from the Bank of Norway informed me that I could have no more dollars. Currency restrictions. I picked up my trunk and took the subway out to Brooklyn. Here I was taken in at the Norwegian Sailors' Home, where the food was good and the prices suited my wallet. I got a little room a floor or two up but had my meals with all the seamen in a big dining room downstairs.

Seamen came and seamen went. They varied in type and dimensions, but they all had one thing in common—when they talked about the sea, they knew what they were talking about. I learned that waves and rough sea did not increase with the depth of the sea or distance from land. On the contrary, squalls were often more treacherous along the coast than in the open sea. Shoal water, backwash along the coast, or ocean currents penned in close to the land could throw up a rougher sea than was usual far out. A vessel which could hold her own along an open coast could hold her own farther out. I also learned that, in a high sea, big ships were inclined to plunge bow or stern into the waves, so that tons of water would rush on board and twist steel tubes like wire, while a small boat, in the same sea, often made good weather because she could find room between the lines of waves and dance freely over them like a gull. I talked

The ancient Indians of Peru did not have boats, but old prints showed that they did build rafts. (From *Spilbergen*, 1614–1617).

to sailors who had got safely away in boats after the seas had made their ship founder.

But the men knew little about rafts. A raft —that wasn't a ship; it had no keel or bulwarks. It was just something floating on which to save oneself in an emergency, until one was picked up by a boat of some kind. One of the men, nevertheless, had great respect for rafts in the open sea; he had drifted about on one for three weeks when a German torpedo sank his ship in mid-Atlantic.

"But you can't navigate a raft," he added. "It goes sideways and backward and round as the wind takes it."

In the library I dug out records left by the first Europeans who had reached the Pacific coast of South America. There was no lack of sketches or descriptions of the Indians' big balsa-wood rafts. They had a square sail and centerboards and a long steering oar astern. So they could be maneuvered.

One Saturday, I marched into a ship chandler's shop down in Water Street. There I was politely addressed as "Captain" when I bought a pilot chart of the Pacific. With the chart rolled up under my arm I took the suburban train out to Ossining, where I was a regular week-end guest of a young Norwegian married couple who had a charming place in the country. My host had been a sea captain and was now office manager for the Fred Olsen Line in New York.

After a refreshing plunge in the swimming pool, we sat down on the lawn in the hot sun. I could contain myself no longer but spread the chart out on the grass and asked Wilhelm if he thought a raft could carry men alive from Peru to the South Sea islands.

He looked at me rather than at the chart, half taken aback, but replied at once in the affirmative. I felt as much lightened as if I had released a balloon inside my shirt, for I knew that to Wilhelm everything that had to do with navigation and sailing was both job and hobby. He was initiated into my plans at once. To my astonishment he then declared that the idea was sheer madness.

"But you said just now that you thought it was possible," I interrupted.

"Quite right," he admitted. "But the chances of its going wrong are just as great. You yourself have never been on a balsa raft, and all of a sudden you're imagining yourself across the Pacific on one. Perhaps it'll come off, perhaps it won't. The old Indians in Peru had generations of experience to build upon. Perhaps ten rafts went to the bottom for every one that got across—or perhaps hundreds in the course of centuries. As you say, the Incas navigated in the open sea with whole flotillas of these balsa rafts. Then, if anything went wrong, they could be picked up by the nearest raft. But who's going to pick you up, out in mid-ocean? Even if you take a radio for use in an emergency, don't think it's going to be easy for a little raft to be located down among the waves thousands of miles from land. In a storm you can be washed off the raft and drowned many times over before anyone gets to you. You'd better wait quietly here till someone has had time to read your manuscript. Write again and stir them up; it's no good if you don't."

"I can't wait any longer now; I shan't have a cent left soon."

"Then you can come and stay with us. For that matter, how can you think of starting an expedition from South America without money?"

"It's easier to interest people in an expedition than in an unread manuscript," I said.

The next week end I was back at Ossining with the chart under my arm. And, when I left, there was a long pencil line from the coast of Peru to the Tuamotu islands in the Pacific.

This Pilot Chart of the Pacific between South America and Polynesia shows how both ocean currents and winds would carry a raft westward. The probable course is marked in red.

(Adapted from U.S. Hydrographic Office Chart)

My friend, the captain, had given up hope of making me drop the idea, and we had sat together for hours working out the raft's probable speed.

"Ninety-seven days," said Wilhelm, "but remember, that's only in theoretically ideal conditions, with a fair wind all the time and assuming that the raft can really sail as you think it can. You must definitely allow at least four months for the trip and be prepared for a good deal more."

"All right," I said optimistically, "let us allow at least four months, but do it in ninety-seven days."

THE EXPLORERS CLUB

On West Seventy-second Street, near Central Park, is one of the most exclusive clubs in New York. There is nothing more than a brightly polished little brass plate with "Explorers Club" on it to tell passers-by that there is anything out of the ordinary inside the doors. But, once inside, one might have made a parachute jump into a strange world, thousands of miles from New York's lines of automobiles flanked by skyscrapers. When the door to New York is shut behind one, one is swallowed up in an atmosphere of lion-hunting, mountaineering, and polar life. Trophies of hippopotamus and deer, big-game rifles, tusks, war drums and spears, Indian carpets, idols and model ships, flags, photographs and maps, surround the members of the club when they assemble for a dinner or to hear lecturers from distant countries.

After my journey to the Marquesas Islands I had been elected an active member of the club, and as junior member I had seldom missed a meeting when I was in town. So, when I now entered the club on a rainy November evening, I was not a little surprised to find the place in an unusual state. In the middle of the floor lay an inflated rubber raft with boat rations and accessories, while parachutes, rubber overalls, safety jackets, and polar equipment covered walls and tables, together with balloons for water distillation, and curious inventions. A newly elected member of the club, Colonel Haskin, of the equipment laboratory of the Air Matériel Command, was to give a lecture and demonstrate a number of new military inventions which, he thought, would in the future be of use to scientific expeditions in both north and south.

After the lecture there was a vigorous discussion. The discussion ended with a surprising offer from Colonel Haskin. Active members of the club could, on their next expeditions, select any they liked of the new inventions he had demonstrated, on the sole condition that they should let his laboratory know what they thought of the things when they came back.

That was that. I was the last to leave the clubrooms that evening. I had to go over every minute detail of all this brand-new equipment which had so suddenly tumbled into my hands and which was at my disposal for the asking. It was exactly what I wanted—equipment with which we could try to save our lives if, contrary to expectation, our wooden raft should show signs of breaking up and we had no other rafts near by.

I FIND A COMPANION

All this equipment was still occupying my thoughts at the breakfast table in the Sailors' Home next morning when a well-dressed young man of athletic build came along with his breakfast tray and sat down at the same

Special survival equipment of the Air Matériel Command included (1) life jacket; (2) device for distilling sea water; (3) rubber life raft; (4) pack with emergency kit; (5) lifeboat rations; (6) sleeping bag.

table as myself. We began to chat, and it appeared that he too was not a seaman but a university-trained engineer from Trondheim. He was living not far away and often had meals at the Sailors' Home because of the good Norwegian cooking there.

He asked me what I was doing, and I then gave him a short account of my plans. I said that, if I did not get a definite answer about my manuscript before the end of the week, I should get under way with the starting of the raft expedition. My table companion did not say much but listened with great interest.

Four days later we ran across each other again in the same dining room.

"Have you decided whether you're going on your trip or not?" he asked.

"Yes," I said. "I'm going."

"When?"

"As soon as possible. If I hang about much longer now, the gales will be coming up from the Antarctic and it will be hurricane season in the islands, too. I must leave Peru in a very few months, but I must get money first and get the whole business organized."

"How many men will there be?"

"I've thought of having six men in all; that'll give some change of society on board the raft and is the right number for four hours' steering in every twenty-four hours."

He stood for a moment or two, as though chewing over a thought, then burst out:

"The devil, but how I'd like to be in it! I could undertake technical measurements and tests. Of course, you'll have to support your experiment with accurate measurements of winds and currents and waves. Remember that you're going to cross vast spaces of sea which are practically unknown because they lie outside all shipping routes. An expedition like yours can make interesting scientific investigations; I could make good use of my scientific knowledge."

I knew nothing about the man beyond what an open face can say. It may say a good deal.

"All right," I said. "We'll go together."

His name was Herman Watzinger; he was as much of a landlubber as myself.

A few days later I took Herman as my guest to the Explorers Club. Here we ran straight into the polar explorer Peter Freuchen. Freuchen had the blessed quality of never disappearing in a crowd. As big as a barn door and bristling with beard, he looked like a messenger from the open tundra. A special atmosphere surrounded him—it was as though he were going about with a grizzly bear on a lead.

We took him over to a big map on the wall and told him about our plan of crossing the Pacific on an Indian raft. His boyish blue eyes grew as large as saucers as he listened. Then he stamped his wooden leg on the floor and tightened his belt several holes.

"Damn it, boys! I should like to go with you!"

The old Greenland traveler began to tell us of his confidence in primitive peoples' watercraft and these peoples' ability to make their way by accommodating themselves to nature both on land and at sea. He himself had traveled by raft down the great rivers of Siberia and towed natives on rafts astern of his ship along the coast of the Arctic. As he talked, he tugged at his beard and said we were certainly going to have a great time.

Through Freuchen's eager support of our plan the wheels began to turn at a dangerous speed, and they soon ran right into the printers' ink of the *Scandinavian Press*. The very next morning there came a violent knocking on my door in the Sailors' Home; I was wanted on the telephone in the passage downstairs. The result of the conversation was that Herman and I, the same evening, rang the doorbell of an apartment in a fashionable quarter of the city. We were received by a well-dressed young man in patent-leather slippers, wearing a silk dressing gown over a blue suit. We knew that this fellow had made a name in America by his exploits as an airman in the war. Besides our host two energetic young journalists, simply bursting with activity and ideas, were present. We knew one of them as an able correspondent.

Our host explained that he was interested in our expedition. He offered to raise the necessary capital if we would undertake to write

Plans being discussed at the Explorers Club in New York. From left to right: Chief of Clannfhearghuis, Herman Watzinger, the author, the polar explorer Peter Freuchen.

newspaper articles and go on lecture tours after our return. We came to an agreement at last. From now on all our economic problems would be solved; they were taken over by our backers and would not trouble us. Herman and I were at once to set about raising a crew and equipment, build a raft, and get off before the hurricane season began.

Next day Herman resigned his job, and we set about our task seriously. I had already obtained a promise from the research laboratory of the Air Matériel Command to send everything I asked for and more through the Explorers Club; they said that an expedition such as ours was ideal for testing their equipment. This was a good start. Our most important tasks were now, first of all, to find four suitable men who were willing to go with us on the raft, and to obtain supplies for the journey.

A party of men who were to put out to sea together on board a raft must be chosen with care. Otherwise there would be trouble and mutiny after a month's isolation at sea. I did not want to man the raft with sailors; they knew hardly any more about managing a raft than we did ourselves, and I did not want to have it argued afterward, when we had completed the voyage, that we made it because we were better seamen than the old raft-builders in Peru. Nevertheless, we wanted one man on board who at any rate could use a sextant and mark our course on a chart as a basis for all our scientific reports.

NOW WE ARE THREE

"I know a good fellow, a painter," I said to Herman. "His name is Erik Hesselberg, and he's a big hefty chap who can play the guitar and is full of fun. He went through navigation school and sailed round the world several times before he settled down at home with brush and palette. I've known him since we were boys and have often been on camping tours with him in the mountains at home. I'll write and ask him; I'm sure he'll come."

"He sounds all right," Herman nodded, "and then we want someone who can manage the radio."

"Radio!" I said, horrified. "What do we want with that? It's out of place on a prehistoric raft."

"Not at all—it's a safety precaution which won't have any effect on your theory so long as we don't send out any SOS for help. And we shall need the radio to send out weather observations and other reports. But it'll be no use for us to receive gale warnings because there are no reports for that part of the ocean, and, even if there were, what good would they be to us on a raft?"

His arguments gradually swamped all my protests, the main ground for which was a lack of affection for push buttons and turning knobs.

"Curiously enough," I admitted, "I happen to have the best connections for getting into touch by radio over great distances with tiny sets. I was put into a radio section in the war. Every man in the right place, you know. But I shall certainly write a line to Knut Haugland and Torstein Raaby."

"Do you know them?"

"Yes. I met Knut for the first time in England in 1944. He'd been decorated by the British for having taken part in the parachute action that held up the German efforts to get the atomic bomb; he was the radio operator, you know, in the 'heavy water' sabotage at Rjukan. When I met him, he had just come back from another job in Norway; the Gestapo had caught him with a secret radio set inside a chimney in the Maternity Clinic in Oslo. Knut fought his way with his pistol from the attic down to the cellar, and from there out into the back yard, where he disappeared over the hospital wall with a hail of bullets after him. I met him at a secret station in an old English castle; he had come back to organize underground liaison among more than a hundred transmitting stations in occupied Norway.

"I myself had just finished my training as a parachutist, and was supposed to jump near Oslo. But when the Russians marched into the Kirkenes region, I was sent instead with a small Norwegian detachment from Scotland to Finnmark to take over the operations, so to speak, from the whole Russian army. And there I met Torstein.

"It was real Arctic winter up in those parts, and the northern lights flashed in the starry sky which was arched over us, pitch black, all day and all night. When we came to the ash heaps of the burned area in Finnmark, frozen blue and wearing furs, a cheery fellow with blue eyes and bristly fair hair crept out of a little hut up in the mountains. This was Torstein Raaby. He had first escaped to England, where he went through special training, and then he'd been smuggled into Norway somewhere near Tromsö. He'd been in hiding with a little transmitting set close to the battleship *Tirpitz* and for ten months he had sent daily reports to England about all that happened on board. It was his reports that guided the British bombers who at last finished off the *Tirpitz*.

Finnmark is part of the northern tip of Norway, where the Northern Lights flash day and night in the black winter sky.

"Torstein escaped to Sweden and from there over to England again, and then he made a parachute jump with a new radio set behind the German lines up in the wilds of Finnmark. When the Germans retreated, he found himself sitting behind our own lines and came out of his hiding place to help us with his little radio, as our main station had been destroyed by a mine. I'm ready to bet that both Knut and Torstein are fed up with hanging about at home now and would be glad to go for a little trip on a wooden raft."

"Write and ask them," Herman proposed.

So I wrote three short letters, to Erik, the painter, Knut, and Torstein:

Am going to cross Pacific on a wooden raft to support a theory that the South Sea islands were peopled from Peru. Will you come? I guarantee nothing but a free trip to Peru and the South Sea islands and back, but you will find good use for your technical abilities on the voyage. Reply at once.

Next day the following telegram arrived: COMING. TORSTEIN.

The other two also accepted.

As sixth member of the party we had in view now one man and now another, but each time some obstacle arose. In the meantime Herman and I had to attack the supply problem. We did not mean to eat llama flesh ,or dried *kumara* potatoes on our trip, for we were not making it to prove that we had once been Indians ourselves. Our intention was to test the performance and quality of the Inca raft, its seaworthiness and loading capacity, and to find out whether the elements would really propel it across the sea to Polynesia with its crew still on board. We were also going to try to find out, on the actual trip, whether they could have obtained additional supplies of fresh fish and rain water while crossing the sea. As our own diet I had thought of simple field service rations, as we knew them from the war.

Just at that time a new assistant to the Norwegian military attaché in Washington had arrived. I had acted as second in command of his company in Finnmark and knew that he was a "ball of fire," who loved to attack and solve with savage energy any problem set before him.

I wrote to Björn Rörholt explaining the situation and asked him to use his tracking sense to smell out a contact man in the supply department of the American army.

Two days later Björn telephoned us from Washington. He had been in contact with the foreign liaison section of the American War Department, and they would like to know what it was all about.

ON TO WASHINGTON

Herman and I took the first train to Washington. We found Björn in his room in the military attaché's office.

"I think it'll be all right," he said. "We'll be

received at the foreign liaison section tomorrow provided we bring a proper letter from the colonel."

The "colonel" was Otto Munthe-Kaas, the Norwegian military attaché. He was well-disposed and more than willing to give us a proper letter of introduction when he heard what our business was.

When we came to fetch the document next morning, he suddenly rose and said he thought it would be best if he came with us himself. We drove out in the colonel's car to the Pentagon building to the offices of the War Department. Soon we were sitting round a large mahogany table at which the head of the foreign liaison section himself presided.

The stern, broad-built West Point officer, who bulked big at the end of the table, had a certain difficulty at first in understanding what the connection between the American War Department and our wooden raft was, but the colonel's well-considered words, and the favorable result of a hurricane-like examination by the officers round the table, slowly brought him over to our side, and he read with interest the letter from the equipment laboratory of the Air Matériel Command. Then he rose and gave his staff a concise order to help us through the proper channels and, wishing us good luck for the present, marched out of the conference room.

The liaison office at once arranged a meeting with Colonel Lewis at the quartermaster general's experimental laboratory, and Herman and I were taken over there by car.

Colonel Lewis was an affable giant of an officer with a sportsman's bearing. He at once called in the men in charge of experiments in the different sections. All were friendly and immediately suggested quantities of equipment they would like us to test thoroughly. They exceeded our wildest hopes as they rattled off the names of nearly everything we could want, from field rations to sunburn ointment and splash-proof sleeping bags. Then they took us on an extensive tour to look at the things. We tasted special rations in smart packings; we tested matches which struck well even if they had been dipped in water, new

primus stoves and water kegs, rubber bags and special boots, kitchen utensils and knives which would float, and all that an expedition could want. Then the tall, friendly colonel suddenly said:

"Well, now we must go in and have a talk with the boss; it's he who'll decide whether we can give you these things."

I felt my heart sink down into my boots. So we were to start our eloquence right from the beginning again, and heaven alone knew what kind of man the "boss" was!

We found that the boss was a little officer with an intensely earnest manner. He sat behind his writing table and examined us with keen blue eyes as we came into the office. He asked us to sit down.

"Well, what do these gentlemen want?" he asked Colonel Lewis sharply, without taking his eyes off mine.

"Oh, a few little things," Lewis hastened to reply. He explained the whole of our errand in outline, while the chief listened patiently without moving a finger.

"And what can they give us in return?" he asked, quite unimpressed.

"Well," said Lewis in a conciliatory tone, "we hoped that perhaps the expedition would be able to write reports on the new provisions and equipment, based on the severe conditions in which they will be using it."

The intensely earnest officer behind the writing table leaned back in his chair with unaffected slowness, with his eyes still fixed on mine, and I felt myself sinking to the bottom of the deep leather chair as he said coolly:

"I don't see at all how they can give us anything in return."

There was dead silence in the room. Colonel Lewis fingered his collar, and neither of us said a word.

"But," the chief suddenly broke out, and now a gleam had come into the corner of his eye, "courage and enterprise count, too. Colonel Lewis, let them have the things!"

I was still sitting, half intoxicated with delight, in the cab which was taking us home to the hotel, when Herman began to laugh and giggle to himself at my side.

"Are you sick?" I asked anxiously.

"No," he laughed shamelessly, "but I've been calculating that the provisions we got include 684 boxes of pineapple, and that's my favorite dish."

There are a thousand things to be done, and mostly at the same time, when six men and a wooden raft and its cargo are to assemble at a place down on the coast of Peru. And we had three months and no Aladdin's lamp at our disposal.

We flew to New York with an introduction from the liaison office and met Professor Behre at Columbia University. He was head of the War Department's Geographical Research Committee, and it was he who pressed the buttons which at last brought Herman all his valuable instruments and apparatus for scientific measurements.

Then we flew to Washington to meet Admiral Glover at the Naval Hydrographic Institute. The good-natured old sea dog called in all his officers and pointed to the chart of the Pacific on the wall as he introduced Herman and me.

"These young gentlemen want to check up on our current maps. Help them!"

When the wheels had rolled a bit further, the English Colonel Lumsden called a conference at the British Military Mission in Washington to discuss our future problems and the chances of a favorable outcome. We received plenty of good advice and a selection of British equipment which was flown over from England to be tried out on the raft expedition. The British medical officer was an enthusiastic advocate of a mysterious shark powder. We were to sprinkle a few pinches of the powder on the water if a shark became too impudent, and the shark would vanish immediately.

"Sir, I said politely, "can we rely on this powder?"

"Well," said the Englishman, smiling, "that's just what we want to find out ourselves!"

MONEY PROBLEMS

When time is short and plane replaces train, while taxi replaces legs, one's wallet crumples up like a withered leaf. When we had spent the cost of my return ticket to Norway, we went and called on our friends and backers in New York to get our finances straight. There we encountered surprising and discouraging problems. The financial manager was ill in bed with fever, and his two colleagues were powerless till he was in action again. We were asked to postpone the business, a useless request, for we could not stop the numerous wheels which were now revolving vigorously. We could only hold on now; it was too late to stop or brake. Our friends the backers agreed to dissolve the whole syndicate in order to give us a free hand to act quickly and independently without them.

So there we were in the street with our hands in our empty trousers pockets.

"December, January, February," said Herman.

"And at a pinch March," said I, "but then we simply must start!"

If nothing else was clear to us at that moment, one thing certainly was. Ours was a journey with an objective, and we did not want to be classed with acrobats who roll down Niagara in empty barrels or sit on the knobs of flag staffs for seventeen days.

"No chewing-gum or pop backing," Herman said.

On this point we were in profound agreement.

We could get Norwegian currency. But that did not solve the problems on our side of the Atlantic. We could apply for a grant from some institution, but we could scarcely get one for a disputed theory; after all, that was just why we were going on the raft expedition. We soon found that neither press nor private promoters dared to put money into what they themselves and all the insurance companies regarded as a suicide voyage; but, if we came back safe and sound, it would be another matter.

Things looked pretty gloomy, and for many days we could see no ray of hope. It was then that Colonel Munthe-Kaas came into the picture again.

"You're in a fix, boys," he said. "Here's a check to begin with. You can return it when you come back from the South Sea islands."

Others followed his example, and my private loan was soon big enough to tide us over without help from agents or others. We could fly to South America and start building the raft.

The old Peruvian rafts were built of balsa wood, which in a dry state is lighter than cork. The balsa tree grows in Peru, but only beyond the mountains in the Andes range, so the seafarers in Inca times went up along the coast to Ecuador, where they felled their huge balsa trees right down on the edge of the Pacific. We meant to do the same.

Today's travel problems are different from those of Inca times. We have cars and planes and travel bureaus but, so as not to make things altogether too easy, we have also impediments called frontiers, with brass-buttoned attendants who doubt one's credentials, maltreat one's luggage, and weigh one down with stamped forms—if one is lucky enough to get in at all. It was the fear of these men with brass buttons that decided us we could not land in South America with packing cases and trunks full of strange devices, raise our hats, and ask politely in broken Spanish to be allowed to come in and sail away on a raft. We should be clapped into jail.

"No," said Herman. "We must have an official introduction."

One of our friends was a correspondent at the United Nations, and he offered to take us out there by car for aid. We were greatly impressed when we came into the great hall of the assembly, where men of all nations sat on benches side by side listening silently to the flow of speech from a black-haired Russian in front of the gigantic map of the world that decorated the back wall.

Our friend the correspondent managed in a quiet moment to get hold of one of the delegates from Peru and, later, one of Ecuador's representatives. On a deep leather sofa in an antechamber they listened eagerly to our plan of crossing the sea to support a theory that men of an ancient civilization from their own country had been the first to reach the Pacific islands. Both promised to inform their governments and guaranteed us support when we came to their respective countries. The assistant secretary of the United Nations, Dr. Benjamin Cohen from Chile, was himself a well-known amateur archaeologist, and he gave me a letter to the President of Peru, who was a personal friend of his. We also met in the hall the Norwegian ambassador, Wilhelm von Munthe of Morgenstierne, who from then on gave the expedition invaluable support.

So we bought two tickets and flew to South America. When the four heavy engines began to roar one after another, we sank into our seats exhausted. We had an unspeakable feeling of relief that the first stage of the program was over and that we were now going straight ahead to the adventure.

Taking the plane for South America marked the real beginning of our adventure.

3. To South America

WE FLEW IN over the South American republic of Ecuador and landed at the tropical port of Guayaquil. We had reached the country where the balsa tree grows and where we would buy timber to build our raft.

The first day we spent in learning the monetary system and enough Spanish to find our way back to the hotel. On the second day we ventured away from our baths in steadily widening circles, and, when Herman had satisfied the longing of his childhood to touch a real palm tree and I was a walking bowl of fruit salad, we decided to go and negotiate for balsa.

Unfortunately this was easier said than done. We could certainly buy balsa in quantities, but not in the form of whole logs, as we wanted it. The days when balsa trees were accessible down on the coast were past. The last war had put an end to them; they had been felled in thousands and shipped to the aircraft factories because the wood was so gaseous and light. We were told that the only place where large balsa trees now grew was in the jungle in the interior of the country.

"Then we must go inland and fell them ourselves," we said.

"Impossible," said the authorities. "The rains have just begun, and all the roads into the jungle are impassable because of flood water and deep mud. If you want balsa wood, you must come back to Ecuador in six months; the rains will be over then and the roads up country will have dried."

In our extremity we called on Don Gustavo von Buchwald, the balsa king of Ecuador, and Herman unrolled his sketch of the raft with the lengths of timber we required. The slight little balsa king seized the telephone eagerly and set his agents to work searching.

In the jungles of Ecuador grow the balsa trees the Indians used for their rafts.

They found planks and light boards and separate short blocks in every sawmill, but they could not find one single serviceable log. There were two big logs, as dry as tinder, at Don Gustavo's own dump, but they would not take us far. It was clear that the search was useless.

"But a brother of mine has a big balsa plantation," said Don Gustavo encouragingly. "His name is Don Federico and he lives at Quevedo, a little jungle town up country. He can get you all you want as soon as we can get hold of him after the rains. It's no use now because of the jungle rain up country."

If Don Gustavo said a thing was no use, all the balsa experts in Ecuador would say it was no use. So here we were in Guayaquil with no timber for the raft and with no possibility of going in and felling the trees ourselves until several months later, when it would be too late.

"Time's short," said Herman.

"And balsa we must have," said I. "The raft must be an exact copy, or we shall have no guarantee of coming through alive."

A little school map we found in the hotel, with green jungle, brown mountains, and inhabited places ringed round in red, told us that the jungle stretched unbroken from the Pacific right to the foot of the towering Andes. I had an idea. It was clearly impracticable now to get from the coastal area through the jungle to the balsa trees at Quevedo, but suppose we could get to the trees from the inland side, by coming straight down into the jungle from the bare snow mountains of the Andes range? Here was a possibility, the only one we saw.

BY AIR TO QUITO

Out on the airfield we found a little cargo plane which was willing to take us up to Quito, the capital of this strange country, high up on the Andes plateau, 9,300 feet above sea level. Between packing cases and furniture we caught occasional glimpses of green jungle and shining rivers before we disappeared into the clouds. When we came out again, the lowlands were hidden under an endless sea of rolling vapor, but ahead of us dry mountainsides

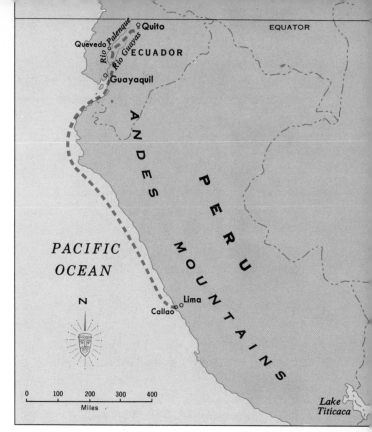

Our search for balsa trees took us from Guayaquil to Quito, and then by jeep over the Andes to Quevedo. The logs were later shipped from Guayaquil to Callao.

and bare cliffs rose from the sea of mist right up to a brilliant blue sky.

The plane climbed straight up the mountainside as in an invisible funicular railway, and, although the Equator itself was in sight, at last we had shining snow fields alongside us. Then we glided between the mountains and over a rich alpine plateau clad in spring green, on which we landed.

Our friend from the cargo plane, Jorge, nicknamed "the crazy flier," belonged to one of the old Spanish families in Quito. He installed us in an antiquated, amusing hotel and then went round, sometimes with and sometimes without us, trying to get us transport over the mountains and down into the jungle to Quevedo. We met in the evening in an old Spanish café, and Jorge was full of bad news; we must absolutely put out of our heads the idea of going to Quevedo. Neither men nor vehicle were to be obtained to take us over the mountains, and certainly not down into the jungle where the rains had begun and where there was danger of attack if one stuck fast in the mud. Only last year a party of ten

American oil engineers had been found killed by poisoned arrows in the eastern part of Ecuador, where many Indians still went about in the jungle stark naked and hunted with poisoned arrows.

Next day we were sitting with our own Consul General Bryhn and his wife under the eucalyptus trees at their big country place outside the town. Bryhn said there were robbers about in those very regions we had thought of visiting. He produced clippings from local papers announcing that soldiers were to be sent out, when the dry season came, to extirpate the *bandidos* who infested the regions around Quevedo. To go there now was the sheerest madness, and we would never get guides or transport. While we were talking to him, we saw a jeep from the American military attaché's office tear past along the road, and this gave us an idea. We went up to the American Embassy, accompanied by the consul general, and were able to see the military attaché himself. He was a trim, lighthearted young man in khaki and riding boots, and he asked laughingly why we had strayed to the top of the Andes when the local papers said we were to go to sea on a wooden raft.

We explained that the wood was still standing upright in the Quevedo jungle and we were up here on the roof of the continent and could not get to it. We asked the military attaché either (*a*) to lend us a plane and two parachutes or (*b*) to lend us a jeep with a driver who knew the country.

The military attaché at first sat speechless at our assurance; then he shook his head despairingly and said with a smile, all right—since we gave him no third choice, he preferred the second!

OVER THE ANDES BY JEEP

At a quarter past five the next morning a jeep rolled up to our hotel entrance, and an Ecuadorian captain of engineers jumped out and reported himself at our service. His orders were to drive us to Quevedo, mud or no mud. The jeep was packed full of gasoline cans, for there were no gasoline pumps or even wheel tracks along the route we were to take.

Our new friend, Captain Agurto Alexis Alvarez, was armed to the teeth with knives and firearms on account of the reports of *bandidos*. We had come to the country peacefully in business suits to buy timber for ready money down on the coast, and the whole of our equipment on board the jeep consisted of a bag of tinned food, except that we had hurriedly acquired a secondhand camera and a pair of tear-proof khaki breeches for each of us. In addition, the consul general had pressed upon us his big revolver with an ample supply of ammunition to exterminate everything that crossed our path. The jeep whizzed away through empty alleys where the moon shone ghostly pale on whitewashed adobe walls, till we came out into the country and raced at a giddy speed along a good sand road southward through the mountain region.

It was good going all along the range as far as the mountain village of Latacunga, where windowless Indian houses clustered blindly round a whitewashed country church with palms in a square. Here we turned off along a mule track which undulated and twisted westward over hill and valley into the Andes. We came into a world we had never dreamed of. It was the mountain Indian's own world—east of the sun and west of the moon —outside time and beyond space. On the whole drive we saw not a carriage or a wheel. The traffic consisted of barelegged goatherds in gaily colored ponchos, driving forward disorderly herds of stiff-legged, dignified llamas, and now and then whole families of Indians coming along the road. The husband usually rode ahead on a mule, while his little wife trotted behind with her entire collection of hats on her head and the youngest child in a bag on her back. All the time she ambled along, she spun wool with her fingers. Donkeys and mules jogged behind at leisure, loaded with boughs and rushes and pottery.

We went on up over sun-smitten slopes without a bush or tree and down into valleys of desert sand and cactus, till finally we climbed up and reached the topmost crest with snow fields round the peak and a wind so bitingly cold that we had to slacken speed in order not to freeze to bits as we sat in our shirts longing for jungle heat. For long stretches we had to drive across country between the mountains, over scree and grassy ridges, searching for the next bit of road. But when we reached the west wall, where the Andes range falls precipitously to the lowlands, the mule track was cut along shelves in the loose rock, and sheer cliffs and gorges were all about us. We put all our trust in friend Agurto as he sat crouched over the steering wheel, always swinging out when we came to a precipice. Suddenly a violent gust of wind met us; we had reached the outermost crest of the Andes chain, where the mountain fell away sharply in a series of precipices to the jungle far down in a bottomless abyss 12,000 feet beneath us. But now our road ran down unhindered into the depths. Always down, in steep loops along gorges and bluffs and ridges, while the air grew damper and warmer and ever fuller of the heavy, deadening hothouse air which rose from the jungle world below.

And then the rain began. First gently, then it began to pour and beat upon the jeep like drumsticks, and soon the chocolate-colored water was flowing down the rocks on every side of us. We almost flowed down, too, away from the dry mountain plateaus behind us and into another world, where stick and stone and clay slope were soft and lush with moss and turf. Leaves shot up; soon they became giant leaves hanging like green umbrellas and dripping over the hillside. There was a gurgling and splashing everywhere. Then the jungle rolled up swiftly like an army of green giant growths that swallowed up the little jeep as it splashed along the waterlogged clay road. The air was moist and warm and heavy with the smell of vegetation.

Mountain Indians and llamas were the only living creatures we met as we crossed the Andes.

IN THE JUNGLE

Darkness had fallen when we reached a cluster of palm-roofed huts on a ridge. Dripping with warm water, we left the jeep for a night under a dry roof. The horde of fleas that attacked us in the hut were drowned in the next day's rain. With the jeep full of bananas and other tropical fruit we went on downhill through the jungle, down and down, though we thought we had reached bottom long ago. The mud grew worse but it did not stop us, and the robbers kept at an unknown distance.

Not till the road was barred by a broad river of muddy water rolling down through the jungle did the jeep give up. We stood stuck fast, unable to move either up or down along the riverbank. In an open clearing stood a hut where a few halfbreed Indians were stretching out a jaguar skin on a sunny wall, while dogs and fowl were splashing about enjoying themselves on top of some cocoa beans spread out to dry in the sun. When the jeep came bumping along, the place came to life and some natives who spoke Spanish informed us that this was the Rio Palenque and that Quevedo was just on the other side. There was no bridge there, and the river was swift and deep, but they were willing to float us and the jeep over by raft. The queer contraption lay down by the bank. Twisted logs as thick as our arms were fastened together with veg-

etable fibers and bamboos to form a flimsy raft, twice the length and breadth of the jeep. With a plank under each wheel and our hearts in our mouths we drove the jeep out onto the logs, and though most of them were submerged under the muddy water, they did bear the jeep and us and four half-naked chocolate-colored men who pushed us off with long poles.

"Balsa?" Herman and I asked together.

"Balsa," one of the fellows nodded, with a disrespectful kick at the logs.

The current seized us and we whirled down the river, while the men pushed in their poles at the right places and kept the raft on an even diagonal course across the current and into quieter water on the other side. This was our first meeting with the balsa tree and our first trip on a balsa raft. We brought the raft safely to land at the farther bank and motored triumphantly into Quevedo. Two rows of tarred wooden houses with motionless vultures on the palm roofs formed a kind of street, and this was the whole place.

AT QUEVEDO

Don Federico's plantation lay a bit farther down the river. When the jeep came bumping into the yard along a path between the mango trees with Agurto, Herman, and me, the lean old jungle-dweller came to meet us at a trot

Our jeep was ferried across the Palenque River on a crude raft of balsa logs.

Felling a balsa tree was not easy, for the ax simply rebounded from the sappy wood.

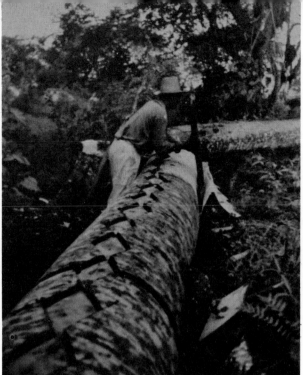

After the trees were felled, the branches were trimmed off and the bark peeled.

with his nephew Angelo, a small boy who lived with him out in the wilds. We gave messages from Don Gustavo, and soon the jeep was standing alone in the yard while a fresh tropical shower streamed down over the jungle. There was a festive meal in Don Federico's bungalow; suckling pigs and chickens crackled over an open fire, while we sat round a dish loaded with tropical fruit and explained what we had come for. The jungle rain pouring down on the ground outside sent a warm sweet gust of scented blossoms and clay in through the window netting.

Don Federico had become as brisk as a boy. Why, yes, he had known balsa rafts since he was a child. Fifty years ago, when he lived down by the sea, the Indians from Peru still used to come sailing up along the coast on big balsa rafts to sell fish in Guayaquil. They could bring a couple of tons of dried fish in a bamboo cabin in the middle of the raft, or they might have wives and children and dogs and fowl on board. Such big balsa trees as they had used for their rafts would be hard to find now in the rains, for floodwater and mud had already made it impossible to get to the balsa plantation up in the forest, even on horseback.

But Don Federico would do his best; there might still be some single trees growing wild in the forest nearer the bungalow, and we did not need many.

Next morning we got up early to go and search for balsa trees.

"Better shake our clothes," said Agurto, and as he spoke a scorpion fell out of his shirt sleeve and shot down into a crack in the floor.

Soon after sunrise Don Federico sent his men out on horseback in all directions to look for accessible balsa trees along the paths. Our own party consisted of Don Federico, Herman, and myself, and we soon found our way to an open place where there was a gigantic old tree of which Don Federico knew. It towered high above the trees round about, and the trunk was three feet thick. In Polynesian style we christened the tree before we touched it; we gave it the name Ku, after a Polynesian deity of American origin. Then we swung the ax and drove it into the balsa trunk till the forest echoed our blows. But cutting a sappy balsa was like cutting cork with a blunt ax; the ax simply rebounded, and I had not delivered many strokes before Herman had to relieve me. The ax changed hands time after time,

33

while the splinters flew and the sweat trickled in the heat of the jungle.

Late in the day Ku was standing like a cock on one leg, quivering under our blows, soon he tottered and crashed down heavily over the surrounding forest, big branches and small trees being pulled down by the giant's fall. We had torn the branches from the trunk and were beginning to rip off the bark in zig-zags in Indian style when Herman suddenly dropped the ax and leaped into the air as if doing a Polynesian war dance, with his hand pressed to his leg. Out of his trouser leg fell a shining ant as big as a scorpion and with a long sting at its tail. It must have had a skull like a lobster's claw, for it was almost impossible to stamp it under one's heel on the ground.

"A kongo," Don Federico explained with regret. "The little brute's worst than a scorpion, but it isn't dangerous to a healthy man."

Herman was tender and sore for several days, but this did not prevent his galloping with us on horseback along the jungle paths, looking for more giant balsas in the forest. From time to time we heard creaking and crashing and a heavy thud somewhere in the virgin forest. Don Federico nodded with a satisfied air. It meant that his half-breed In-dians had felled a new giant balsa for the raft. In a week Ku had been followed by Kane, Kama, Ilo, Mauri, Ra, Rangi, Papa, Taranga, Kura, Kukara, and Hiti—twelve mighty balsas, all christened in honor of Polynesian legendary figures whose names had once been borne with Tiki over the sea from Peru. The logs, glistening with sap, were dragged down through the jungle first by horses and at the last by Don Federico's tractor, which brought them to the riverbank in front of the bunga-low.

The sap-filled logs were far from being as light as corks. They must have weighed a ton apiece, and we waited with great anxiety to see how they would float in the water. We rolled them out to the edge of the bank one by one; there we made fast a rope of tough, climbing plants to the ends of the logs that they might not vanish downstream when we let them enter the water. Then we rolled them in turn down the bank and into the river. There was a mighty splash. They swung round and floated, about as much above as below the surface of the water, and when we went out along them they remained steady. We bound the timbers together with tough lianas that hung down from the tops of the jungle trees, so as to make two temporary

The big balsa logs were bound together to make rafts that could be floated downstream.

Meals were cooked by our Indian compan-ions over a little fire on the raft.

rafts, one towing the other. Then we loaded the rafts with all the bamboos and lianas we should need later, and Herman and I went on board with two men of a mysterious mixed race, with whom we had no common language.

DOWN THE PALENQUE BY RAFT

When we cut our moorings, we were caught by the whirling masses of water and went off downstream at a good pace. The last glimpse we had in the drizzle, as we rounded the first headland, was of our excellent friends standing on the end of the point in front of the bungalow, waving. Then we crept under a little shelter of green banana leaves and left steering problems to the two brown experts who had stationed themselves one in the bow and one astern, each holding a huge oar. They kept the raft in the swiftest current with ease, and we danced downstream on a winding course between sunken trees and sandbanks.

When mealtimes came, we relieved our friends at the steering oars while they fried fish and breadfruit over a little fire regulated with wet clay. Roast chicken, eggs, and tropical fruits were also part of the menu on board, while the logs transported themselves and us at a fine speed down through the jungle toward the sea. When darkness fell upon the river we crawled inside the hut and went to sleep. What did it matter now if the water swept and splashed round us? The more it rained, the swifter the current ran.

The farther downstream we drifted, the thicker became the huts and native plantations, and soon there were regular villages on the banks. The traffic here consisted of dugout canoes punted along with long poles, and now and then we saw a little balsa raft loaded with heaps of green bananas bound for market.

Where the Palenque joined the Rio Guayas, the water had risen so high that the paddle steamer was plying busily between Vinces and Guayaquil down on the coast. To save valuable time Herman and I each got a hammock on board the paddle steamer and steamed off across the thickly populated flat country to the coast. Our brown friends were to follow, drifting down alone with the timber.

At Guayaquil Herman and I parted. He was to remain at the mouth of the Guayas to stop the balsa logs as they came drifting down. Thence he was to take them, as cargo on a coasting steamer, to Peru, where he was to direct the building of the raft and make a faithful copy of the Indians' old-time vessels. I myself took the regular plane southward to Lima, the capital of Peru, to find a suitable place for building the raft.

PORT OF CALLAO

On my arrival in Lima I took the street car down to the port of Callao to find a place where we could build the raft. I saw at once that the whole harbor was chock-full of ships and cranes and warehouses, with customs sheds and harbor offices and all the rest. And, if there was any open beach farther out, it swarmed with bathers to such a degree that inquistive people would pull the raft and fittings to pieces as soon as our backs were turned. Callao was now the most important port in a country of seven million people, white and brown. Times had changed for raft-builders in Peru even more than in Ecuador, and I saw only one possibility—to get inside the high concrete walls round the naval har-

A hut covered with banana leaves gave shelter from both rain and sun.

35

bor, where armed men stood on guard behind the iron gate and cast menacing and suspicious looks on me and other unauthorized persons who loafed past the walls. If one could only get in there, one would be safe.

I had met the Peruvian naval attaché in Washington and had a letter from him to support me. I went to the Ministry of Marine next day with the letter and sought an audience with the minister of marine, Manuel Nieto. He received in the morning in the elegant Empire drawing room of the Ministry, gleaming with mirrors and gilding. After a time he himself came in in full uniform, a short, broadly built officer, as stern as Napoleon, straightforward and concise in his manner of speech. He asked why and I said why. I asked to be allowed to build a wooden raft in the naval dockyard.

"Young man," said the minister, drumming uneasily with his fingers, "you've come in by the window instead of the door. I'll be glad to help you, but the order must come from the foreign minister to me; I can't let foreigners into the naval area and give them the use of the dockyard as a matter of course. Apply to the Foreign Ministry in writing, and good luck."

I thought apprehensively of papers circulating and disappearing into the blue. Happy were the rude days of Kon-Tiki, when applications were an unknown hindrance!

To see the foreign minister in person was considerably harder. Norway had no local legation in Peru, and our helpful Consul General Bahr could, therefore, take me no farther than the counselors of the Foreign Ministry. I was afraid things would get no further. Dr. Cohen's letter to the President of the republic might come in useful now. So I sought through his adjutant an audience of His Excellency Don José Bustamante y Rivero, president of Peru. A day or two later I was told to be at the palace at twelve o'clock.

Lima is a modern city, with half a million inhabitants, and lies spread over a green plain at the foot of the desert mountains. The president's palace stands in the middle of the city and is strongly guarded by armed sentries in gaily colored costumes. An audience in Peru is a serious business, and few people have seen the president except on the screen. After registering, I was taken into one room by a man in white, then to a much handsomer room where I was greeted by a man in a gold-edged uniform. He took me into a large, gilded room, splendidly decorated and with gilded furniture, and left me alone. Then came another and still another imposing gentleman in uniform who told me that the President sent me his greetings and would be free very soon when a meeting of ministers was over.

Ten minutes later steady steps once more broke the silence, and this time a man with gold lace and epaulets came in. I sprang briskly from the sofa and bowed deeply. The man bowed still more deeply and led me through several rooms and up a staircase with thick carpets. Then he left me in a tiny little room with a simple leather-covered chair and a sofa. In came a little man in a white suit, who greeted me amiably and remained standing. This was President Bustamante y Rivero.

WITH THE PRESIDENT IN PERU

The President had twice as much English as I had Spanish, so when we had greeted one another and he had begged me with a gesture to sit down, our common vocabulary was exhausted. Signs and gesticulations will do a lot, but they will not get one permission to build a raft in a naval harbor in Peru. The only thing I perceived was that the President did not understand what I was saying, and he grasped that still more clearly himself, for in a little while he disappeared and came back with the air minister, General Reveredo. The general spoke English splendidly with an American accent.

I apologized for the misunderstanding and said it was not to the airfield that I had been trying to ask for admission but to the naval harbor. The general laughed and explained that he had only been called in as interpreter. Bit by bit the theory was translated to the President, who listened closely and put sharp questions through General Reveredo. At last he said:

"If it is possible that the Pacific islands were first discovered from Peru, Peru has an interest in this expedition. If we can do anything for you, tell us."

I asked for a place where we could build the raft within the walls of the naval area, access to the naval workshops, a place for the storage of equipment and facilities for bringing it into the country, the use of the dry dock and of naval personnel to help us in the work, and a vessel to tow us out from the coast when we started.

"What is he asking for?" the President asked eagerly, so that I too understood.

"Nothing much," Reveredo answered, looking at me with a twinkle in his eye. And the President, satisfied, nodded as a sign of approval.

Before the meeting broke up, Reveredo promised that the foreign minister should receive orders from the President personally, and that Minister of Marine Nieto should be given a free hand to give us all the help we had asked for.

"God preserve you all!" said the General, laughing and shaking his head. The adjutant came in and escorted me out to a waiting messenger.

That day the Lima papers published a paragraph about the Norwegian raft expedition which was to start from Peru; at the same time they announced that a Swedish-Finnish scientific expedition had finished its studies among the jungle Indians in the Amazon regions. Two of the Swedish members of the Amazon expedition had come on up the river by canoe to Peru and had just arrived in Lima. One was Bengt Danielsson, from Uppsala University, who was now going to study the mountain Indians in Peru.

I cut out the paragraph, and was sitting in my hotel writing to Herman about the site for building the raft, when I was interrupted by a knock on the door. In came a tall sun-

The president's palace in Lima is a handsome building on one side of the Plaza de Armas.

All six members of the expedition finally met in Lima. From left to right: Knut Haugland, Bengt Danielsson, the author, Erik Hesselberg, Torstein Raaby, Herman Watzinger.

burned fellow in tropical clothes, and, when he took off his white helmet, it looked as if his flaming red beard had burned his face and scorched his hair thin. That fellow came from the wilds, but his place was clearly a lecture room.

"Bengt Danielsson," I thought.

"Bengt Danielsson," said the man, introducing himself.

I asked him to sit down.

"I've just heard of the raft plans," said the Swede. "And now I've come to ask if I may come with you. I'm interested in the migration theory."

I knew nothing about the man except that he was a scientist and that he had come straight out of the depths of the jungle. But if a solitary Swede had the pluck to go out on a raft with five Norwegians, he could not be squeamish. And not even that imposing beard could hide his placid nature and gay humor.

NOW WE ARE SIX

Bengt became the sixth member of the crew, for the place was still vacant. And he was the only one who spoke Spanish.

The passenger plane droned northward along the coast a few days later with me on board en route to Washington, D.C. Soon we six were to be packed together like invisible microbes on a mere speck, down there where there was so much water that it looked as if it overflowed all along the western horizon. We would not be able to get more than a few steps away from one another. For the time being, at any rate, there was elbow room enough between us. Herman was in Ecuador waiting for the timber. Knut Haugland and

Torstein Raaby had just arrived in New York by air. Erik Hesselberg was on board ship from Oslo, bound for Panama, and Bengt was in the hotel at Lima ready to start, waiting to meet the others.

No two of these men had met before, and they were all of entirely different types. That being so, we would be on the raft for some weeks before we got tired of one another's stories. No storm clouds or gusty weather were any more dangerous than the cloudbursts that might occur among six men shut up together for months on a drifting raft. In such circumstances a good joke was often as valuable as a life belt.

BACK IN WASHINGTON

Up in Washington there was still bitter winter weather when I came back—cold and snowy February. Björn had tackled the radio problem and had interested the Radio Amateur League of America in listening in for reports from the raft. Knut and Torstein were busy preparing the transmission, which was to be done partly with short-wave transmitters specially constructed for our purpose and partly with secret sabotage sets used during the war. There were a thousand things to prepare, big and small, if we were to do all that we planned on the voyage.

Laws and regulations tied our hands everywhere, and knot after knot had to be loosened in turn.

Then one day a telegram came from Lima. Herman had been caught in the backwash of a breaker and flung ashore, badly injured, with his neck dislocated. He was under treatment in Lima Hospital.

Torstein Raaby was sent down by air at once with Gerd Vold, the popular London secretary of the Norwegian parachute saboteurs in the war, who was now helping us in Washington. They found Herman better; he had been hung up by a strap round his head for half an hour while the doctors twisted the atlas vertebra in his neck back into position. The X-ray picture showed that the highest bone in his neck was cracked and had been turned right around. Herman's splendid con-

dition had saved his life, and he was soon back, blue and green and stiff and rheumatic, in the naval dockyard, where he had assembled the balsa wood and started the work. He had to remain in the doctor's hands for several weeks, and it was doubtful whether he would be able to make the voyage with us. He himself never doubted it for a moment, despite his initial rough handling in the embrace of the Pacific.

Then Erik arrived by air from Panama and Knut and I from Washington, and so we were all assembled at the starting point in Lima.

Down in the naval dockyard lay the big balsa logs from the Quevedo forest. It was really a pathetic sight. Fresh-cut round logs, yellow bamboos, reeds, and green banana leaves lay in a heap, our building materials, in between rows of threatening gray submarines and destroyers. Six fair-skinned northerners and twenty brown Peruvian seamen with Inca blood in their veins swung axes and long machete knives and tugged at ropes and knots. Trim naval officers in blue and gold walked over and stared in bewilderment at these pale strangers and their crude vegetable materials which had suddenly appeared in the midst of their proud naval yard.

WE BUILD THE RAFT

For the first time for hundreds of years a balsa raft was being built in Callao Bay. In these coastal waters, where Inca legends affirm that their ancestors first learned to sail such rafts from Kon-Tiki's vanished clan, modern Indians were forbidden to build such rafts by men of our own race. Sailing on an open raft can cost human lives. The descendants of the Incas have moved with the times; like us, they have creases in their trousers and are safely protected by the guns of their naval craft. Bamboo and balsa belong to the primitive past; here, too, life is marching on—to armor and steel.

The ultramodern dockyard gave us wonderful support. With Bengt as interpreter and Herman as chief constructor we had the run of the carpenter's and sailmaker's shops, as well as half the storage space as a dump for our

Building the raft in Callao Harbor. We first lashed the nine balsa logs together with ordinary hemp rope. No nails or metal was used.

equipment and a small floating pier where the timber was put into the water when the building began.

Nine of the thickest logs were chosen as sufficient to form the actual raft. Deep grooves were cut in the wood to prevent the ropes which were to fasten them and the whole raft together from slipping. Not a single spike, nail, or wire rope was used in the whole construction. The nine great logs were first laid loose side by side in the water so that they might all fall freely into their natural floating position before they were lashed securely together. The longest log, 45 feet long, was laid in the middle and projected a long way at both ends. Shorter and shorter logs were laid symmetrically on both sides of this, so that the sides of the raft were 30 feet long and the bow stuck out like a blunt plow. Astern the raft was cut off straight across, except that the three middle logs projected and supported a short thick block of balsa wood which lay athwart ship and held tholepins for the long steering oar. When the nine balsa logs were lashed securely together with separate lengths of inch-and-a-quarter hemp rope, the lighter balsa logs were made fast crossways over them at intervals of about 3 feet.

The raft itself was now complete, laboriously fastened together with about three hundred different lengths of rope, each firmly knotted. A deck of split bamboos was laid upon it, fastened to it in the form of separate strips and covered with loose mats of plaited bamboo reeds. In the middle of the raft, but nearer the stern, we erected a small open cabin of bamboo canes, with walls of plaited bamboo reeds and a roof of bamboo slats with leathery banana leaves overlapping one another like tiles. Forward of the cabin we set up two masts side by side. They were cut from mangrove wood, as hard as iron, and leaned toward each other, so that they were lashed together crosswise at the top. The big rectangular square sail was hauled up on a yard made of two bamboo stems bound together to secure double strength.

The nine big logs of timber which were to carry us over the sea were pointed at their forward ends in native fashion that they might glide more easily through the water, and quite low splashboards were fastened to the bow above the surface of the water.

At various places, where there were large chinks between the logs, we pushed down in all five solid fir planks which stood on their edges in the water under the raft. They were scattered about without system and went down 5 feet into the water, being 1 inch thick and 2 feet wide. They were kept in place with

Lighter balsa logs were placed crossways over the big logs and lashed fast in place.

A deck of split bamboos, a small cabin, and two masts lashed together at the top completed our raft.

wedges and ropes and served as tiny parallel keels or centerboards. Centerboards of this kind were used on all the balsa rafts of Inca times, long before the time of the discoveries, and were meant to prevent the flat wooden rafts from drifting sideways with wind and sea. We did not make any rail or protection round the raft, but we had a long slim balsa log which afforded foothold along each side.

The whole construction was a faithful copy of the old vessels in Peru and Ecuador except for the low splashboards in the bow, which later proved to be entirely unnecessary. After finishing the raft itself, of course, we could arrange the details on board as we liked, so long as they had no effect on the movement and quality of the vessel. We knew that this raft was to be our whole world in the time that lay before us and that, consequently, the smallest detail on board would increase in dimensions and importance as the weeks passed.

Therefore we gave the little deck as much variation as possible. The bamboo strips did not deck in the whole raft but formed a floor forward of the bamboo cabin and along the starboard side of it where the wall was open. The port side of the cabin was a kind of back yard full of boxes and gear made fast, with a narrow edge left to walk along. Forward in the bow, and in the stern as far as the after wall of the cabin, the nine gigantic logs were not decked in at all. So, when we moved round the bamboo cabin, we stepped from yellow bamboos and wickerwork down on to the round gray logs astern and up again on to piles of cargo on the other side. It was not many steps, but the psychological effect of the irregularity gave us variation and compensated us for our limited freedom of movement. Up at the masthead we placed a wooden platform, not so much in order to have a lookout post, when at last we came to land, as to be able to clamber up while en route and look at the sea from another angle.

WARNINGS

When the raft began to take shape and lay there among the warships, golden and fresh with ripe bamboos and green leaves, the minister of marine himself came to inspect us. We were immensely proud of our vessel as she lay there, a brave little reminder of Inca times among the threatening big warships. But the minister of marine was utterly horrified by what he saw. I was summoned to the naval office to sign a paper freeing the Navy from all responsibility for what we had built in its harbor, and to the harbor master to sign a paper saying that, if I left the harbor with men and cargo on board, it was entirely on my own responsibility and at my own risk.

Later a number of foreign naval experts and diplomats were admitted to the dockyard to see the raft. They were no more encouraging, and a few days afterward I was sent for by the ambassador of one of the Great Powers.

As a private individual he begged me to give up the voyage while there was yet time.

41

1. 9 Main Balsa Logs
2. 9 Cross Logs
3. 2 Long Side Logs
4. 2 Spars Forming Mast
5. Block of Balsa Holding Tholepins
6. Short Pieces to Fill Gaps
7. Top Mast
8. Steering Oar
9. Tholepins
10. Topmast Platform
11. Centerboards
12. Oar Blade
13. Splashboards
14. Bow Log
15. Crosstree
16. Bow Struts
17. Flag and Radio Mast
18. Bamboo Yard
19. Long Pieces of Bamboo
20. Split Bamboo Matting
21. Cabin
22. Banana Leaf Roof Cover
23. Canvas Sail
24. Rope Ladder
25. Radio Antenna

This diagram shows the details of the construction of the raft.

An admiral who had inspected the raft had told him that we should never get across alive. In the first place, the raft's dimensions were wrong. It was so small that it would founder in a big sea; at the same time it was just long enough to be lifted up by two lines of waves at the same time, and with the raft filled with men and cargo the fragile balsa logs would break under the strain. And, what was worse, the biggest balsa exporter in the country had told him that the porous balsa logs would float only a quarter of the distance across the sea

before they became so completely water-logged that they would sink under us.

This sounded bad but, as we stuck to our guns, we were given a Bible as a present to take with us on our voyage. All in all, there was little encouragement to be had from the experts who looked at the raft. Gales and perhaps hurricanes would wash us overboard and destroy the low, open craft, which would simply lie helpless and drift in circles about the ocean before wind and sea. Even in an ordinary choppy sea we should be continually

Comparison of the diagram on p. 42 with this old print shows how faithfully the *Kon-Tiki* was copied after the Indian balsa rafts of Ecuador and Peru. (From *Humboldt*, 1810).

drenched with salt water which would take the skin off our legs and ruin everything on board. If we added up all that the different experts, each in turn, had pointed out as the vital flaw in the construction itself, there was not a length of rope, not a knot, not a measurement, not a piece of wood in the whole raft which would not cause us to founder at sea. High wagers were made as to how many days the raft would last, and a flippant naval attaché bet all the whiskey the members of the expedition could drink for the rest of their lives if they reached the South Sea islands alive.

Worst of all was when a Norwegian ship came into port and we took the skipper and one or two of his most experienced sea dogs into the dockyard. We were eager to hear their practical reactions. And our disappointment was great when they all agreed that the blunt-bowed, clumsy craft would never get any help from the sail, while the skipper maintained that, if we kept afloat, the raft would take a year or two to drift across with the Humboldt Current. The boatswain looked at our lashings and shook his head. We need not worry. The raft would not hold together for a fortnight before every single rope was worn through, for when at sea the big logs would be continually moving up and down and rubbing against one another. Unless we used wire ropes or chains, we might as well pack up.

These were difficult arguments to stifle. If only one of them proved to be right, we had not a chance. I am afraid I asked myself many times if we knew what we were doing. I could not counter the warnings one by one myself because I was not a seaman. But I had in reserve one single trump in my hand, on which the whole voyage was founded. I knew all the time in my heart that a prehistoric civilization had been spread from Peru and across to the islands at a time when rafts like ours were the only vessels on that coast. And I drew the general conclusion that, if balsa wood had floated and lashings held for Kon-Tiki in 500 A.D., they would do the same for us now if we blindly made our raft an exact copy of his. Bengt and Herman had gone into the theory most thoroughly, and, while the experts lamented, all the boys took the thing quite calmly and had a royal time in Lima.

A few days before we sailed, provisions and water and all our equipment were stowed on board the raft. We took provisions for six men for four months, in the form of solid little cardboard cartons containing military rations. Herman had the idea of boiling asphalt and pouring it so as to make a level layer round each separate carton. Then we strewed sand on the cartons, to prevent them from sticking together, and stowed them, packed close, under the bamboo deck where they filled the space between the nine low crossbeams which supported the deck.

At a crystal-clear spring high up in the mountains we filled fifty-six small water cans with 275 gallons of drinking water. These, too, we made fast in between the crossbeams so that the sea might always splash round them. On the bamboo deck we lashed fast the rest of the equipment, including large wicker baskets full of fruit, roots, and coconuts.

Knut and Torstein took one corner of the bamboo cabin for the radio, and inside the hut, down between the crossbeams, we made fast eight boxes. Two were reserved for scientific instruments and films; the other six were allotted one to each of us, with an intimation that each man could take with him as much private property as he could find room for in his own box. As Erik had brought several rolls of drawing paper and a guitar, his box was so full that he had to put his stockings in Torstein's. It took four seamen to carry Bengt's box on board. He brought nothing but books. We laid plaited reed mats and our straw mattresses on top of the boxes and then we were ready to start.

First, the raft was towed out of the naval area and paddled round in the harbor for a while to see if the cargo was stowed evenly. Then she was towed across to the Callao Yacht Club, where invited guests and other persons interested were to be present at the naming of the raft the day before we sailed.

NAMING OF THE RAFT

On April 27, 1947, the Norwegian flag was hoisted. Along a yard at the masthead waved the flags of the foreign countries which had given the expedition practical support. The quay was packed with people who wanted to see the strange craft christened. There were swarms of journalists and a clicking of movie cameras; indeed, the only things that were lacking were a brass band and a big drum. One thing was quite clear to us all— if the raft went to pieces outside the bay, we would paddle to Polynesia, each of us on a log, rather than dare come back here again.

Gerd Vold, the expedition's secretary and contact on the mainland, was to christen the raft with milk from a coconut, partly to be in harmony with the Stone Age and partly because, owing to a misunderstanding, the champagne had been put at the bottom of Torstein's private box. When our friends had been told in English and Spanish that the raft was named after the Incas' great forerunner— the sun-king who had vanished westward over the sea from Peru and appeared in Polynesia 1,500 years ago—Gerd Vold christened the raft *Kon-Tiki*. She smashed the coconut (previously cracked) so hard against the bow that milk and bits of coconut filled the hair of all those who stood reverently around.

Then the bamboo yard was hauled up and the sail shaken out, with Kon-Tiki's bearded head, painted in red by our artist Erik, in its center. It was a faithful copy of the sun-king's head cut in red stone on a statue in the ruined city of Tiahuanaco.

The completed raft in Callao Harbor, ready to begin the voyage to Polynesia. On April 27, 1947, the raft was formally christened and given the name of *Kon-Tiki*.

Fish of a multitude of sizes, shapes, and colors live in the Pacific Ocean.

4. Out to Sea

THERE WAS A BUSTLE in Callao Harbor the day the *Kon-Tiki* was to be towed out to sea. The minister of marine had ordered the naval tug *Guardian Rios* to tow us out of the bay and cast us off clear of the coastal traffic, out where in times gone by the Indians used to lie fishing from their rafts. The papers had published the news under both red and black headlines, and there was a crowd of people down on the quays from early in the morning of April 28.

We six who were to assemble on board all had little things to do at the eleventh hour, and when I came down to the quay, only Herman was there keeping guard over the raft. I intentionally stopped the car a long way off and walked the whole length of the mole to stretch my legs thoroughly for the last time for no one knew how long. I jumped on board the raft, which looked an utter chaos of banana clusters, fruit baskets, and sacks which had been hurled on board at the very last moment and were to be stowed and made fast. In the middle of the heap Herman sat resignedly holding on to a cage with a green parrot in it, a farewell present from a friendly soul in Lima.

"Look after the parrot a minute," said Herman. "I must go ashore and have a last glass of beer. The tug won't be here for hours."

He had hardly disappeared among the swarm on the quay when the people began to point and wave. And around the point at full speed came the tug *Guardian Rios*. She dropped anchor on the farther side of a waving forest of masts which blocked the way in to the *Kon-Tiki* and sent in a large motorboat to tow us out between the sailing craft. She was packed full of seamen, officers, and movie photographers, and, while orders rang out and cameras clicked, a stout towrope was made fast to the raft's bow.

"*Un momento*," I shouted in despair from where I sat with the parrot. "It's too early; we must wait for the others—*los expedicionarios*," I explained and pointed toward the city.

But nobody understood. The officers only smiled politely, and the knot at our bow was made fast in more than exemplary manner. I cast off the rope and flung it overboard with all manner of signs and gesticulations. The parrot utilized the opportunity afforded by all the confusion to stick its beak out of the cage and turn the knob of the door, and when I turned round it was strutting cheerfully about the bamboo deck. I tried to catch it, but it shrieked rudely in Spanish and fluttered away over the banana clusters. With one eye on the sailors who were trying to cast a rope over the bow I started a wild chase after the parrot. It fled shrieking into the bamboo cabin, where I got it into a corner and caught it by one leg as it tried to flutter over me. When I came out again and stuffed my flapping trophy into its cage, the sailors on land had cast off the raft's moorings, and we were dancing helplessly in and out with the backwash of the long swell that came rolling in over the mole. In despair I seized a paddle and vainly tried to parry a violent bump as the raft was flung against the wooden piles of the quay. Then the motorboat started, and with a jerk the *Kon-Tiki* began her long voyage.

My only companion was a Spanish-speaking parrot which sat glaring sulkily in a cage. People on shore cheered and waved, and the swarthy movie photographers in the motorboat almost jumped into the sea in their eagerness to catch every detail of the expedition's dramatic start from Peru. Despairing and alone I stood on the raft looking out for my lost companions, but none appeared. So we came out to the *Guardian Rios*, which was lying with steam up ready to lift anchor and start. I was up the rope ladder in a twinkling and made so much row on board that the start was postponed and a boat sent back to the quay. It was away a good while, and then it came back full of pretty señoritas but without a single one of the *Kon-Tiki's* missing men. This was all very well but it did not solve my problems, and, while the raft swarmed with charming señoritas, the boat went back on a fresh search for *los expedicionarios noruegos*.

Meanwhile Erik and Bengt came sauntering down to the quay with their arms full of reading matter and odds and ends. They met the whole stream of people on its way home and were finally stopped at a police barrier by a kindly official who told them there was nothing more to see. Bengt told the officer, with an airy gesture of his cigar, that they had not come to see anything; they themselves were going with the raft.

"It's no use," the officer said indulgently. "The *Kon-Tiki* sailed an hour ago."

"Impossible," said Erik, producing a parcel. "Here's the lantern!"

"And there's the navigator," said Bengt, "and I'm the steward."

They forced their way past, but the raft had gone. They trotted desperately to and fro along the mole where they met the rest of the party, who also were searching eagerly

Our parrot escaped from its cage and fluttered about the deck, adding to the confusion.

Towed by the *Guardian Rios*, the *Kon-Tiki* left Callao Harbor on April 28. Head seas made the raft buck and roll at the end of its rope.

for the vanished raft. Then they caught sight of the boat coming in, and so we were all six finally united and the water was foaming round the raft as the *Guardian Rios* towed us out to sea.

It had been late in the afternoon when at last we started, and the *Guardian Rios* would not cast us off till we were clear of the coastal traffic next morning. Directly we were clear of the mole we met a bit of a head sea, and all the small boats which were accompanying us turned back one by one. Only a few big

yachts came with us out to the entrance of the bay to see how things would go out there.

A BAD START

The *Kon-Tiki* followed the tug like an angry billy goat on a rope, and she butted her bow into the head sea so that the water rushed on board. This did not look very promising, for this was a calm sea compared with what we had to expect. In the middle of the bay the towrope broke, and our end of it sank peacefully to the bottom while the tug steamed ahead. We flung ourselves down along the side of the raft to fish for the end of the rope, while the yachts went on and tried to stop the tug. Stinging jellyfish as thick as wash-tubs splashed up and down with the seas alongside the raft and covered all the ropes with a slippery, stinging coating of jelly. When the raft rolled one way, we hung flat over the side waving our arms down toward the surface of the water, until our fingers just touched the slimy towrope. Then the raft rolled back again, and we all stuck our heads deep down into the sea, while salt water and giant jellyfish poured over our backs. We spat and cursed and pulled jellyfish fibers out of our hair, but when the tug came back the rope end was up and ready for splicing.

When we were about to throw it on board the tug, we suddenly drifted in under the vessel's overhanging stern and were in danger of being crushed against her by the pressure of the water. We dropped everything we had and tried to push ourselves clear with bamboo sticks and paddles before it was too late. But we never got a proper position, for when we were in the trough of the sea we could not reach the iron roof above us, and when the water rose again the *Guardian Rios* dropped her whole stern down into the water and would have crushed us flat if the suction had carried us underneath. Up on the tug's deck people were running about and shouting; at last the propeller began to turn alongside us, and it helped us clear of the backwash under the *Guardian Rios* in the last second. The bow of the raft had had a few hard knocks and had become a little crooked in the lashings, but this fault rectified itself by degrees.

"When a thing starts so damnably, it's bound to end well," said Herman. "If only this towing could stop; it'll shake the raft to bits."

The towing went on all night at a slow speed and with only one or two small hitches. The yachts had bidden us farewell long ago, and the last coast light had disappeared astern. Only a few ships' lights passed us in the darkness. We divided the night into watches to keep an eye on the towrope, and we all had a good snatch of sleep. When it grew light next morning, a thick mist lay over the coast of Peru, while we had a brilliant blue sky ahead of us to westward. The sea was running in a long quiet swell covered with little white crests, and clothes and logs and everything we took hold of were soaking wet with dew. It was chilly, and the green water round us was astonishingly cold for 12° south.

We were in the Humboldt Current, which carries its cold masses of water up from the Antarctic and sweeps them north all along the coast of Peru till they swing west and out across the sea just below the Equator. It was out here that Pizarro, Zárate, and the other early Spaniards saw for the first time the Inca Indians' big sailing rafts, which used to go out for 50 to 60 sea miles to catch tunnies and dolphins in the same Humboldt

Fifty sea miles out from land, we said good-by to the *Guardian Rios*.

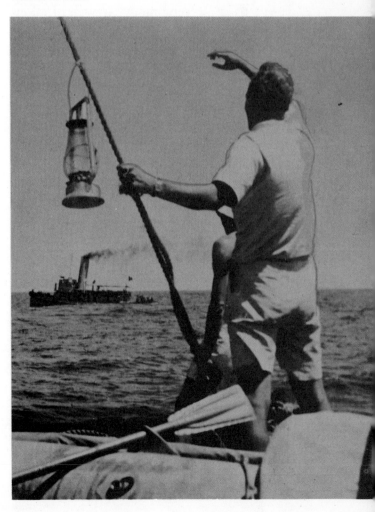

Current. All day long there was an offshore wind out here, but in the evening the onshore wind reached as far out as this and helped the rafts home if they needed it.

In the early light we saw our tug lying close by, and we took care that the raft lay far enough away from her bow while we launched our little inflated rubber dinghy. It floated on the waves like a football and danced away with Erik, Bengt, and myself till we caught hold of the *Guardian Rios*' rope ladder and clambered on board. With Bengt as interpreter we had our exact position shown us on our chart. We were 50 sea miles from land in a northwesterly direction from Callao, and we were to carry lights the first few nights so as not to be sunk by coasting ships. Farther out we would not meet a single ship, for no shipping route ran through that part of the Pacific.

FAREWELL

We took a ceremonious farewell of all on board, and many strange looks followed us as we climbed down into the dinghy and went tumbling back over the waves to the *Kon-Tiki*. Then the towrope was cast off and the raft was alone again. Thirty-five men on board the *Guardian Rios* stood at the rail waving for as long as we could distinguish outlines. And six men sat on the boxes on board the *Kon-Tiki* and followed the tug with their eyes as long as they could see her. Not till the black column of smoke had dissolved and vanished over the horizon did we shake our heads and look at one another.

"Good-by, good-by," said Torstein. "Now we'll have to start the engine, boys!"

We laughed and felt the wind. There was a rather light breeze, which had veered from south to southeast. We hoisted the bamboo yard with the big square sail. It only hung down slack, giving Kon-Tiki's face a wrinkled, discontented appearance.

"It looks as if we were losing ground," said Herman, and he threw a piece of balsa wood overboard at the bow.

"One-two-three . . . thirty-nine, forty."

The piece of balsa wood still lay quietly in the water alongside the raft; it had not yet moved halfway along our side.

"We'll have to go over with it," said Torstein optimistically.

"Hope we don't drift astern with the evening breeze," said Bengt. "It was great fun saying good-by at Callao, but I'd just as soon miss our welcome back again!"

Now the piece of wood had reached the end of the raft. We shouted hurrah and began to stow and make fast all the things that had been flung on board at the last moment. Bengt set up a primus stove at the bottom of an empty box, and soon we were regaling ourselves on hot cocoa and biscuits and making a hole in a fresh coconut. The bananas were not quite ripe yet.

"We're well off now in one way," Erik chuckled. He was rolling about in wide sheepskin trousers under a huge Indian hat, with the parrot on his shoulder. "There's only one thing I don't like," he added, "and that's all the little-known crosscurrents which can fling us right upon the rocks along the coast if we go on lying here like this."

We considered the possibility of paddling but agreed to wait for a wind.

THE WIND COMES

And the wind came. It blew up from the southeast quietly and steadily. Soon the sail filled and bent forward like a swelling breast, with Kon-Tiki's head bursting with pugnacity. And the *Kon-Tiki* began to move. We shouted westward ho! and hauled on sheets and ropes. The steering oar was put into the water, and the watch roster began to operate. We threw balls of paper and chips of wood overboard at the bow and stood aft with our watches.

"One, two, three . . . . eighteen, nineteen —now!"

Paper and chips passed the steering oar and soon lay like pearls on a thread, dipping up and down in the trough of the waves astern. We went forward yard by yard. The *Kon-Tiki* did not plow through the sea like a sharp-prowed racing craft. Blunt and broad, heavy and solid, she splashed sedately forward over the waves. She did not hurry, but when she had once got going she pushed ahead with unshakeable energy.

At the moment the steering arrangements were our greatest problem. The raft was built exactly as the Spaniards described it, but there was no one living in our time who could give us a practical advance course in sailing an Indian raft. The problem had been thoroughly discussed among the experts on shore but with meager results. They knew just as little about it as we did. As the southeasterly wind increased in strength, it was necessary to keep the raft on such a course that the sail was filled from astern. If the raft turned her side too much to the wind, the sail suddenly swung round and banged against cargo and men and bamboo cabin, while the whole raft turned round and continued on the same course stern first. It was a hard struggle, three men fighting

Early Spanish explorers saw Inca Indians sailing their big balsa rafts far out in the Humboldt Current.

Our steering oar was 19 feet long and was made of tough mangrove wood. The oar blade was lashed on with rope.

with the sail and three others rowing with the long steering oar to get the nose of the wooden raft round and away from the wind. And, as soon as we got her round, the steersman had to take good care that the same thing did not happen again the next minute.

The steering oar, nineteen feet long, rested loose between two tholepins on a large block astern. It was the same steering oar our native friends had used when we floated the timber down the Palenque in Ecuador. The long mangrove-wood pole was as tough as steel but so heavy that it would sink if it fell overboard. At the end of the pole was a large oar blade of fir wood lashed on with ropes. It took all our strength to hold this long steering oar steady when the seas drove against it, and our fingers were tired out by the convulsive grip which was necessary to turn the pole so that the oar blade stood straight up in the water. This last problem was finally solved by our lashing a crosspiece to the handle of the steering oar so that we had a sort of lever to turn. And meanwhile the wind increased.

By the late afternoon the trade wind was already blowing at full strength. It quickly stirred up the ocean into roaring seas which swept against us from astern. For the first time we fully realized that here was the sea itself come to meet us; it was bitter earnest now— our communications were cut. Whether things went well now would depend entirely on the balsa raft's good qualities in the open sea. We knew that, from now onward, we should never get another onshore wind or chance of turning back. We were in the path of the real trade wind, and every day would carry us farther and farther out to sea. The only thing to do was to go ahead under full sail; if we tried to turn homeward, we should only drift farther out to sea stern first. There was only one possible course, to sail before the wind with our bow toward the sunset. And, after all, that was the object of our voyage—to follow the sun in its path as we thought Kon-Tiki and the old sun-worshipers must have done when they were driven out to sea from Peru.

FIGHTING THE WAVES

We noted with triumph and relief how the wooden raft rose up over the first threatening wave crests that came foaming toward us. But it was impossible for the steersman to hold the oar steady when the roaring seas rolled toward him and lifted the oar out of the tholepins, or swept it to one side so that the steersman was swung round like a helpless acrobat. Not even two men at once could hold the oar steady when the seas rose against us and pounded down over the steersmen aft. We hit on the idea of running ropes from the oar blade to each side of the raft; and with other ropes holding the oar in place in the tholepins it obtained a limited freedom of movement and could defy the worst seas if only we ourselves could hold on.

As the troughs of the sea gradually grew deeper, it became clear that we had moved into the swiftest part of the Humboldt Current. This sea was as obviously caused by a current and not simply raised by the wind. The water was green and cold and everywhere about us; the jagged mountains of Peru had vanished into the dense cloudbanks astern. When darkness crept over the waters, our first duel with the elements began. We were still not sure of the sea; we were still uncertain whether it would show itself a friend or an enemy in the intimate proximity we ourselves had sought. When, swallowed up by the darkness, we heard the general noise from the sea

View astern from the mast, showing the steersman and steering oar. Thousands of tons of water poured in astern daily and vanished between the logs.

around us suddenly deafened by the hiss of a roller close by and saw a white crest come groping toward us on a level with the cabin roof, we held on tight and waited uneasily to feel the masses of water smash down over us and the raft.

But every time there was the same surprise and relief. The *Kon-Tiki* calmly swung up her stern and rose skyward unperturbed, while the masses of water rolled along her sides. Then we sank down again into the trough of the waves and waited for the next big sea. The biggest seas often came two or three in succession, with a long series of smaller seas in between. It was when two big seas followed each other too closely that the second broke on board aft, because the first was still holding our bow in the air. It became, therefore, an unbreakable law that the steering watch must have ropes round their waists, the other ends of which were made fast to the raft, for there were no bulwarks. Their task was to keep the sail filled by holding stern to sea and wind.

We had made an old boat's compass fast to a box aft so that Erik could check our course and calculate our position and speed. For the time being it was uncertain where we were, for the sky was overclouded and the horizon one single chaos of rollers. Two men at a time took turns as steering watch and, side by side, they had to put all their strength into the fight with the leaping oar, while the rest of us tried to snatch a little sleep inside the open bamboo cabin.

When a really big sea came, the men at the helm left the steering to the ropes and, jumping up, hung on to a bamboo pole from the cabin roof, while the masses of water thundered in over them from astern and disappeared between the logs or over the side of the raft. Then they had to fling themselves at the oar again before the raft could turn round and the sail thrash about. For, if the raft took the seas at an angle, the waves could easily pour right into the bamboo cabin. When they came from astern, they disappeared between the projecting logs at once and seldom came so far forward as the cabin wall. The round logs astern let the water pass as if through the

prongs of a fork. The advantage of a raft was obviously this: the more leaks the better. Through the gaps in our floor the water ran out but never in.

About midnight a ship's light passed in a northerly direction. At three another passed on the same course. We waved our little paraffin lamp and hailed them with flashes from an electric torch, but they did not see us and the lights passed slowly northward into the darkness and disappeared. Little did those on board realize that a real Inca raft lay close to them, tumbling among the waves. And just as little did we on board the raft realize that this was our last ship and the last trace of men we should see till we had reached the other side of the ocean.

We clung like flies, two and two, to the steering oar in the darkness and felt the fresh sea water pouring off our hair while the oar hit us till we were tender both behind and before and our hands grew stiff with the exertion of hanging on. We had a good schooling those first days and nights; it turned landlubbers into seamen. For the first twenty-four hours every man, in unbroken succession, had two hours at the helm and three hours' rest. We arranged that every hour a fresh man should relieve one of the two steersmen who had been at the helm for two hours.

Every single muscle in the body was strained to the uttermost throughout the watch to cope with the steering. When we were tired out with pushing the oar, we went over to the other side and pulled, and when arms and chest were sore with pressing, we turned our backs while the oar kneaded us green and blue in front and behind. When at last the relief came, we crept half-dazed into the bamboo cabin, tied a rope round our legs, and fell asleep with our salty clothes on before we could get into our sleeping bags. Almost at the same moment there came a brutal tug at the rope; three hours had passed, and one had to go out again and relieve one of the two men at the steering oar.

The next night was still worse; the seas grew higher instead of going down. Two hours on end of struggling with the steering

We divided the day and night into steering watches of two hours for each man. The steersman always had a rope about his waist so that he would not be swept overboard by a big wave.

With a good wind the *Kon-Tiki* danced over the waves like a cork steam roller. No matter how the seas foamed and rolled, the raft slid easily over them.

oar was too long; a man was not much use in the second half of his watch, and the seas got the better of us and hurled us round and sideways, while the water poured on board. Then we changed over to one hour at the helm and an hour and a half's rest. So the first sixty hours passed, in one continuous struggle against a chaos of waves that rushed upon us, one after another, without cessation. High waves and low waves, pointed waves and round waves, slanting waves and waves on top of other waves.

The one of us who suffered worst was Knut. He was let off steering watch, and suffered silent agonies in a corner of the cabin. The parrot sat sulkily in its cage, hanging on with its beak and flapping its wings every time the raft gave an unexpected pitch and the sea splashed against the wall from astern. The *Kon-Tiki* did not roll excessively. She took the seas more steadily than any boat of the same dimensions, but it was impossible to predict which way the deck would lean each time, and we never learned the art of moving about

the raft easily, for she pitched as much as she rolled.

On the third night the sea went down a bit, although it was still blowing hard. About four o'clock an unexpected deluge came foaming through the darkness and knocked the raft right round before the steersmen realized what was happening. The sail thrashed against the bamboo cabin and threatened to tear both the cabin and itself to pieces. All hands had to go on deck to secure the cargo and haul on sheets and stays in the hope of getting the raft on her right course again, so that the sail might fill and curve forward peacefully. But the raft would not right herself. She would go stern foremost, and that was all. The only result of all our hauling and pushing and rowing was that two men nearly went overboard in a sea when the sail caught them in the dark.

The sea had clearly become calmer. Stiff and sore, with skinned palms and sleepy eyes, we were not worth a row of beans. Better to save our strength in case the weather should call us out to a worse passage of arms. One

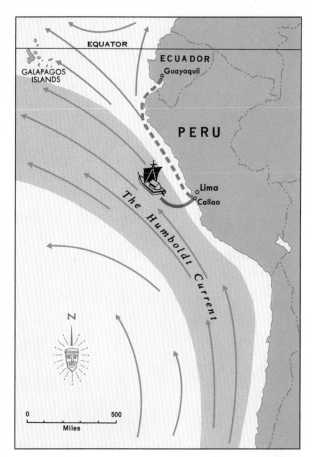

The Humboldt Current sweeps north along the coast of Peru and then swings west into the Pacific. This was the course the *Kon-Tiki* must follow to reach Polynesia.

if the seas foamed and rose high so long as they only left us in peace on the raft? What did it matter if they rose straight up in front of our noses when we knew that in a second the raft would go over the top and flatten out the foaming ridge like a steam roller, while the heavy, threatening mountain of water only lifted us up in the air and rolled groaning and gurgling under the floor? The old masters from Peru knew what they were doing when they avoided a hollow hull which could fill with water, or a vessel so long that it would not take the waves one by one. A cork steam roller—that was what the balsa raft amounted to.

Erik took our position at noon and found that, in addition to our run under sail, we had made a big deviation northward along the coast. We still lay in the Humboldt Current just 100 sea miles from land. The great question was whether we would get into the treacherous eddies south of the Galapagos Islands. This could have fatal consequences, for up there we might be swept in all directions by strong ocean currents making toward the coast of Central America. But, if things went as we calculated, we should swing west across the sea with the main current before we got as far north as the Galapagos. The wind was still blowing straight from southeast. We hoisted the sail, turned the raft stern to sea, and continued our steering watches.

PLANE MISSES US

Knut had now recovered from the torments of seasickness, and he and Torstein clambered up to the swaying masthead, where they experimented with mysterious radio aerials which they sent up both by balloon and by kite. Suddenly one of them shouted from the radio corner of the cabin that he could hear the naval station at Lima calling us. They were telling us that the American ambassador's plane was on its way out from the coast to bid us a last good-by and see what we looked like at sea. Soon after we obtained direct contact with the operator in the plane and then a completely unexpected chat with the secretary to the expedition, Gerd Vold, who was on board.

could never know. So we furled the sail and rolled it round the bamboo yard. The *Kon-Tiki* lay sideways on to the seas and took them like a cork. Everything on board was lashed fast, and all six of us crawled into the little bamboo cabin, huddled together, and slept like mummies in a sardine tin.

We little guessed that we had struggled through the hardest steering of the voyage. Not till we were far out on the ocean did we discover the Inca's simple and ingenious way of steering a raft.

We did not wake till well on in the day, when the parrot began to whistle and halloo and dance to and fro on its perch. Outside the sea was still running high but in long, even ridges and not so wild and confused as the day before. The first thing we saw was that the sun was beating down on the yellow bamboo deck and giving the sea all round us a bright and friendly aspect. What did it matter

Beneath Kon-Tiki's bearded face. The head on the sail was copied from a stone carving of the legendary sun-king Virakocha or Kon-Tiki (see p. 15).

We gave our position as exactly as we could and sent direction-finding signals for hours. The voice in the ether grew stronger and weaker as ARMY-119 circled round near and far and searched. But we did not hear the drone of the engines and never saw the plane. It was not easy to find the low raft down in the trough of the seas, and our own view was strictly limited. At last the plane had to give it up and returned to the coast. It was the last time anyone tried to search for us.

The sea ran high in the days that followed, but the waves came hissing along from the southeast with even spaces between them and the steering went more easily. We took the sea and wind on the port quarter, so that the steersman got fewer seas over him and the raft went more steadily and did not swing round. We noted anxiously that the southeast trade wind and the Humboldt Current were, day after day, sending us straight across on a course leading to the countercurrents round the Galapagos Islands. And we were going due northwest so quickly that our daily average in those days was 55 to 60 sea miles, with a record of 71 sea miles in one day.

We were now so accustomed to having the sea dancing round us that we took no account of it. What did it matter if we danced round a bit with a thousand fathoms of water under us, so long as we and the raft were always on top? It was only that here the next question arose—how long could we count on keeping on top? It was easy to see that the balsa logs

The underside of the raft, showing how the ropes gradually wore their way into the logs.

absorbed water. The aft crossbeam was worse than the others; on it we could press our whole finger tip into the soaked wood till the water squelched. Without saying anything I broke off a piece of the sodden wood and threw it overboard. It sank quietly beneath the surface and slowly vanished down into the depths. Later I saw two or three of the other fellows do exactly the same when they thought no one was looking. They stood silently looking at the waterlogged piece of wood sinking quietly into the green water.

We had noted the water line on the raft when we started, but in the rough sea it was impossible to see how deep we lay, for one moment the logs were lifted out of the water and the next they went deep down into it. But, if we drove a knife into the timber, we saw to our joy that the wood was dry an inch or so below the surface. We calculated that, if the water continued to force its way in at the same pace, the raft would be lying and floating just under the surface of the water by the time we could expect to be approaching land. But we hoped that the sap further in would act as an impregnation and check the absorption.

WOOD AGAINST ROPES

Then there was another menace which troubled our minds a little during the first weeks. The ropes. In the daytime we were so busy that we thought little about it, but, when darkness had fallen and we had crept into bed on the cabin floor, we had more time to think, feel, and listen. As we lay there, each man on his straw mattress, we could feel the reed matting under us heaving in time with the wooden logs. In addition to the movements of the raft itself, all nine logs moved reciprocally. When one came up, another went down with a gentle heaving movement. They did not move much, but it was enough to make one feel as if one were lying on the back of a large breathing animal, and we preferred to lie on a log lengthways. The first two nights were the worst, but then we were too tired to bother about it. Later the ropes swelled a little in the water and kept the nine logs quieter.

But all the same there was never a flat surface on board which kept quite still in relation to its surroundings. As the foundation moved up and down and round at every joint, everything else moved with it. The bamboo deck, the double mast, the four plaited walls of the cabin, and the roof of slats with the leaves on it—all were made fast just with ropes and twisted about and lifted themselves in opposite directions. It was almost unnoticeable but it was evident enough. If one corner went up, the other corner came down, and if one half of the roof dragged all its laths forward, the other half dragged its laths astern. And, if we looked out through the open wall, there was still more life and movement, for there the sky moved quietly round in a circle while the sea leaped high toward it.

Knut goes down to inspect the lashings on the raft's bottom. The author holds him by the ankles.

The ropes took the whole pressure. All night we could hear them creaking and groaning, chafing and squeaking. It was like one single complaining chorus round us in the dark, each rope having its own note according to its thickness and tautness.

Every morning we made a thorough inspection of the ropes. We were even let down with our heads in the water over the edge of the raft, while two men held us tight by the ankles, to see if the ropes on the bottom of the raft were all right. But the ropes held. A fortnight, the seamen had said. Then all the ropes would be worn out. But, in spite of this consensus of opinion, we had not so far found the smallest sign of wear. Not till we were far out to sea did we find the solution. The balsa wood was so soft that the ropes wore their way slowly into the wood and were protected, instead of the logs wearing the ropes, as had been predicted.

After a week or so the sea grew calmer, and we noticed that it became blue instead of green. We began to go west-northwest instead of due northwest and took this as the first faint sign that we had got out of the coastal current and had some hope of being carried out to sea.

The very first day we were left alone on the sea we had noticed fish round the raft, but we were too much occupied with the steering to think of fishing. The second day we went right into a thick shoal of sardines, and soon afterward an eight-foot blue shark came along and rolled over with its white belly uppermost as it rubbed against the raft's stern, where Herman and Bengt stood barelegged in the seas, steering. It played round us for a while but disappeared when we got the hand harpoon ready for action.

Next day we were visited by tunnies, bonitos, and dolphins, and when a big flying fish thudded on board we used it as bait and at once pulled in two large dolphins (dorados) weighing from twenty to thirty-five pounds each. This was food for several days. On steering watch we could see many fish we did not even know, and one day we came into a school of porpoises which seemed quite endless. The black backs tumbled about, packed close together, right in to the side of the raft, and sprang up here and there all over the sea as far as we could see from the masthead. And the nearer we came to the Equator, and the farther from the coast, the commoner flying fish became. When at last we came out into the blue water where the sea rolled by majestically, sunlit and serene, ruffled by gusts of wind, we could see them glittering like a rain of projectiles which shot from the water and flew in a straight line till their power of flight was exhausted and they vanished beneath the surface.

FLYING FISH FOR MEALS

If we set the little paraffin lamp out at night, flying fish were attracted by the light and, large and small, shot over the raft. They often struck the bamboo cabin or the sail and tumbled helpless on the deck. Unable to get a take-off by swimming through the water, they just remained lying and kicking helplessly, like large-eyed herrings with long breast fins. They always came at a good pace and snout first, and if they caught one full in the face they made it burn and tingle. But the unprovoked attack was quickly forgiven by the injured party, for, with all its drawbacks, we were in a land of enchantment where delicious

A bout with a tunny was exciting sport. There were fish enough in the sea to feed a whole fleet of rafts.

Herman with a bonito. It sometimes happened that bonitos swam on board with the waves.

fish dishes came hurling through the air. We used to fry them for breakfast, and whether it was the fish, the cook, or our appetites, they reminded us of fried troutlings once we had scraped the scales off.

The cook's first duty, when he got up in the morning, was to go out on deck and collect all the flying fish that had landed on board in the course of the night. There were usually half a dozen or more, and once we found twenty-six fat flying fish on the raft. Knut was much upset one morning because, when he was standing operating with the frying pan, a flying fish struck him on the hand instead of landing right in the cooking fat.

Our neighborly intimacy with the sea was not fully realized by Torstein till he woke one morning and found a sardine on his pillow. There was so little room in the cabin that Torstein had to lie with his head in the doorway, and, if anyone inadvertently trod on his face when going out at night, he bit him in the leg. He grasped the sardine by the tail and confided to it understandingly that all sardines had his entire sympathy. We conscientiously drew in our legs so that Torstein should have more room the next night, but then something happened which caused Torstein to find himself a sleeping place on top of all the kitchen utensils in the radio corner.

The cook's first duty in the morning was to collect all the flying fish which had landed on deck during the night.

A MIDNIGHT VISITOR

It was a few nights later. It was overcast and pitch dark, and Torstein had placed the paraffin lamp close by his head, so that the night watches could see where they were treading when they crept in and out over his head. About four o'clock Torstein was awakened by the lamp tumbling over, and something cold and wet flapped about his ears. "Flying fish," he thought and felt for it in the darkness to throw it away. He caught hold of something long and wet, which wriggled like a snake, and let go as if he had burned himself. The unseen visitor twisted itself away and over to Herman, while Torstein tried to get the lamp lighted again. Herman started up, too, and this made me wake, thinking of the squid which came up at night in these waters.

When we got the lamp lighted, Herman was sitting in triumph with his hand gripping the neck of a long thin fish which wriggled in his hands like an eel. The fish was over three feet long, as slender as a snake, with dull black eyes and a long snout with a greedy jaw full of long sharp teeth. The teeth were as sharp as knives and could be folded back into the roof of the mouth to make way for what was swallowed. Under Herman's grip a large-eyed white fish, about eight inches long, was suddenly thrown up from the stomach and out of the mouth of the predatory fish, and soon after up came another like it. These were clearly two deep-water fish, much torn by the snakefish's teeth. The snakefish's thin skin was a bluish violet on the back and steel blue underneath, and it came loose in flakes when we took hold of it.

A rare and unusual deep-sea fish, the snake mackerel, leaped on board one night and found its way into Torstein's sleeping bag, with upsetting results.

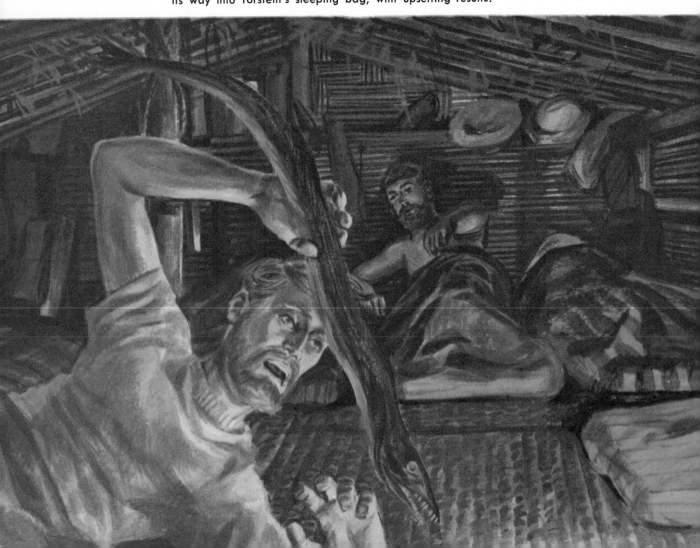

Bengt too was awakened at last by all the noise, and we held the lamp and the long fish under his nose. He sat up drowsily in his sleeping bag and said solemnly:

"No, fish like that don't exist."

With which he turned over quietly and fell asleep again.

Bengt was not far wrong. It appeared later that we six sitting round the lamp in the bamboo cabin were the first men to have seen this fish alive. Only the skeleton of a fish like this one had been found a few times on the coast of South America and the Galapagos Islands; scientists called it *Gempylus*, or snake mackerel, and thought it lived at the bottom of the sea at a great depth because no one had ever seen it alive. But, if it lived at a great depth, it must have done so by day when the sun blinded its big eyes. For on dark nights it was abroad high over the surface of the sea; we on the raft had experience of that.

The sea contains many surprises for him who has his floor on a level with the surface and drifts along slowly and noiselessly. A sportsman who breaks his way through the woods may come back and say that no wild life is to be seen. Another may sit down on a stump and wait, and often rustlings and cracklings will begin and curious eyes peer out. So it is on the sea, too. We usually plow across it with roaring engines and piston strokes, with the water foaming round our bow. Then we come back and say that there is nothing to see far out on the ocean.

Not a day passed but we, as we sat floating on the surface of the sea, were visited by inquisitive guests which wriggled and waggled about us, and a few of them, such as dolphins and pilot fish, grew so familiar that they accompanied the raft across the sea and kept round us day and night.

When night had fallen and the stars were twinkling in the dark tropical sky, a phosphorescence flashed around us in rivalry with the stars, and single glowing plankton resembled round live coals so vividly that we involuntarily drew in our bare legs when the glowing pellets were washed up round our feet at the raft's stern. When we caught them, we saw

The *Gempylus,* or snake mackerel, looked like a snake and had long, sharp teeth. We were the first to see a live specimen of this strange fish.

that they were little brightly shining species of shrimp. On such nights we were sometimes scared when two round shining eyes suddenly rose out of the sea right alongside the raft and glared at us with an unblinking hypnotic stare. The visitors were often big squids which came up and floated on the surface with their devilish green eyes shining in the dark like phosphorus. But sometimes the shining eyes were those of deep-water fish which came up only at night and lay staring, fascinated by the glimmer of light before them. Several times, when the sea was calm, the black water round the raft was suddenly full of round heads two or three feet in diameter, lying motionless and staring at us with great glowing eyes. On other nights balls of light three feet and more in diameter would be visible down in the water, flashing at irregular intervals like electric lights turned on for a moment.

We gradually grew accustomed to having these subterranean or submarine creatures under the floor, but nevertheless we were just as surprised every time a new species appeared. About two o'clock on a cloudy night, when the man at the helm had difficulty in distinguishing black water from black sky, he caught sight of a faint illumination down in the water which slowly took the shape of a large animal. It was impossible to say whether it was plankton shining on its body, or whether the animal itself had a phosphorescent surface, but the glimmer down in the black water gave the ghostly creature obscure, wavering outlines. Sometimes it was roundish, sometimes oval, or triangular, and suddenly it split into two parts which swam to and fro under the raft independently of each other. Finally there were three of these large shining phantoms wandering round in slow circles under us.

They were real monsters, for the visible parts alone were some five fathoms long, and we all quickly collected on deck and followed the ghost dance. It went on for hour after hour, following the course of the raft. Mysterious and noiseless, our shining companions kept a good way beneath the surface, mostly on the starboard side where the light was, but often they were right under the raft or appeared on the port side. The glimmer of light on their backs revealed that the beasts were bigger than elephants but they were not whales, for they never came up to breathe. Were they giant ray fish which changed shape when they turned over on their sides? They took no notice at all if we held the light right down on the surface to lure them up, so that we might see what kind of creatures they were. And, like all proper goblins and ghosts, they had sunk into the depths when the dawn began to break.

THE WORLD'S BIGGEST FISH

We never got a proper explanation of this nocturnal visit from the three shining monsters, unless the solution was afforded by another visit we received a day and a half later in the full midday sunshine. It was May 24, and we were lying drifting on a leisurely swell in exactly 95° west by 7° south. It was about noon, and we had thrown overboard the guts of two big dolphins we had caught earlier in the morning. I was having a refreshing plunge overboard at the bow, lying in the water but keeping a good lookout and hanging on to a rope end, when I caught sight of a thick brown fish, six feet long, which came swimming inquisitively toward me through the crystal-clear sea water. I hopped quickly up on to the edge of the raft and sat in the hot sun

The monstrous whale shark is the largest known fish—and one of the ugliest. It may range from 40 to 60 feet in length.

looking at the fish as it passed quietly, when I heard a wild war whoop from Knut, who was sitting aft behind the bamboo cabin. He bellowed "Shark!" till his voice cracked in a falsetto, and, as we had sharks swimming alongside the raft almost daily without creating such excitement, we all realized that this must be something extra-special and flocked astern to Knut's assistance.

Knut had been squatting there, washing his pants in the swell, and when he looked up for a moment he was staring straight into the biggest and ugliest face any of us had ever seen in the whole of our lives. It was the head of a veritable sea monster, so huge and so hideous that, if the Old Man of the Sea himself had come up, he could not have made such an impression on us. The head was broad and flat like a frog's, with two small eyes right at the sides, and a toadlike jaw which was four or five feet wide and had long fringes drooping from the corners of the mouth. Behind the head was an enormous body ending in a long thin tail with a pointed tail fin which stood straight up and showed that this sea monster was not any kind of whale. The body looked brownish under the water, but both head and body were thickly covered with small white spots.

The monster came quietly, lazily swimming after us from astern. It grinned like a bulldog and lashed gently with its tail. The large round dorsal fin projected clear of the water and sometimes the tail fin as well, and, when the creature was in the trough of the swell, the water flowed about the broad back as though washing round a submerged reef. In front of the broad jaws swam a whole crowd of zebra-striped pilot fish in fan formation, and large remora fish and other parasites sat firmly attached to the huge body and traveled with it through the water, so that the whole thing looked like a curious zoological collection crowded round something that resembled a floating deep-water reef.

A twenty-five-pound dolphin, attached to six of our largest fishhooks, was hanging behind the raft as bait for sharks, and a swarm of pilot fish shot straight off, nosed the dolphin without touching it, and then hurried back to their lord and master, the sea king. Like a mechanical monster it set its machinery going and came gliding at leisure toward the dolphin which lay, a beggarly trifle, before its jaws. We tried to pull the dolphin in, and the sea monster followed slowly, right up to the side of the raft. It did not open its mouth but just let the dolphin bump against it, as if to throw open the whole door for such an insignificant scrap was not worth while. When the giant came close up to the raft, it rubbed its back against the heavy steering oar, which was just lifted up out of the water, and now we had ample opportunity of studying the monster at the closest quarters—at such close quarters that I thought we had all gone mad, for we roared stupidly with laughter and shouted over-excitedly at the completely fantastic sight we saw. Even a cartoonist could not have created a more incredibly ugly monster.

The monster was a whale shark, the largest shark and the largest fish known in the world today. It is exceedingly rare, but scattered specimens are observed here and there in the tropical oceans. The whale shark has an average length of fifty feet, and according to zoologists it weighs fifteen tons. It is said that large specimens can attain a length of sixty feet; one harpooned baby had a liver weighing six hundred pounds and a collection of three thousand teeth in each of its broad jaws.

Our monster was so large that, when it began to swim in circles round us and under the raft, its head was visible on one side while the whole of its tail stuck out on the other. And so incredibly grotesque, inert, and stupid did it appear when seen fullface that we could not help shouting with laughter, although we realized that it had strength enough in its tail to smash both balsa logs and ropes to pieces if it attacked us. Again and again it described narrower and narrower circles just under the raft, while all we could do was wait and see what might happen. When it appeared on the other side, it glided amiably under the steering oar and lifted it up in the air, while the oar blade slid along the creature's spotted back.

We stood round the raft with hand harpoons ready for action, but they seemed to us like toothpicks in relation to the mammoth beast we had to deal with. There was no indication that the whale shark ever thought of leaving us again; it circled round us and followed like a faithful dog, close up to the raft. None of us had ever experienced or thought we should experience anything like it; the whole adventure, with the sea monster swimming behind and under the raft, seemed to us so completely unnatural that we could not really take it seriously.

In reality the whale shark went on encircling us for barely an hour, but to us the visit seemed to last a whole day. At last it became too exciting for Erik, who was standing at a corner of the raft with an eight-foot hand harpoon, and, encouraged by ill-considered shouts, he raised the harpoon above his head. As the whale shark came gliding slowly toward him and its broad head moved right under the corner of the raft, Erik thrust the harpoon with all his giant strength down between his legs and deep into the whale shark's gristly head. It was a second or two before the giant understood properly what was happening. Then in a flash the placid half-wit was transformed into a thrashing mountain of steel muscles.

We heard a swishing noise as the harpoon line rushed over the edge of the raft and saw a cascade of water as the giant stood on its head and plunged down into the depths. The three men who were standing nearest were flung about the place, head over heels, and two of them were flayed and burned by the line as it rushed through the air. The thick line, strong enough to hold a boat, was caught up on the side of the raft but snapped at once like a piece of twine, and a few seconds later a broken-off harpoon shaft came up to the surface two hundred yards away. A shoal of frightened pilot fish shot off through the water in a desperate attempt to keep up with their old lord and master. We waited a long time for the monster to come racing back like an infuriated submarine, but we never saw anything more of him.

SEA-TURTLE HUNT

We were now in the South Equatorial Current and moving in a westerly direction just 400 sea miles south of the Galapagos. There was no longer any danger of drifting into the Galapagos currents, and the only contacts we had with this group of islands were greetings from big sea turtles which no doubt had strayed far out to sea from the islands. One day we saw a thumping turtle lying struggling with its head and one great fin above the surface of the water. As the swell rose, we saw a shimmer of green and blue and gold in the water under the turtle, and we discovered that it was engaged in a life-and-death struggle with dolphins. The fight was apparently quite one-sided; it consisted in twelve to fifteen big-headed, brilliantly colored dolphins attacking the turtle's neck and fins and apparently trying to tire it out, for the turtle could not lie for days on end with its head and paddles drawn inside its shell.

When the turtle caught sight of the raft, it dived and made straight for us, pursued by the glittering fish. It came close up to the side of the raft and was showing signs of wanting to climb up on to the timber when it caught sight of us already standing there. If we had been more practiced, we could have captured it with ropes without difficulty as the huge carapace paddled quietly along the side of the raft. But we spent the time that mattered in staring, and when we had the lasso ready the giant turtle had already passed our bow. We flung the little rubber dinghy into the water, and Herman, Bengt, and Torstein went in pursuit of the turtle in the round nutshell, which was not a great deal bigger than what swam ahead of them. Bengt, as steward, saw in his mind's eye endless meat dishes and a most delicious turtle soup.

But the faster they rowed, the faster the turtle slipped through the water just below the surface, and they were not more than a hundred yards from the raft when the turtle suddenly disappeared without a trace. But they had done one good deed at any rate. For when the little yellow rubber dinghy came dancing back over the water, it had the whole glittering school of dolphins after it. They circled round the new turtle, and the boldest snapped at the oar blades which dipped into the water like fins; meanwhile, the peaceful turtle escaped successfully from all its ignoble persecutors.

Occasionally we saw a big sea turtle that had strayed out to sea from the Galapagos Islands.

Toward Polynesia in sunny weather. With the help of ocean currents and trade winds we moved westward at an average speed of about 42½ sea miles per day.

5. Halfway

THE WEEKS PASSED. We saw no sign either of a ship or of drifting remains to show that there were other people in the world. The whole sea was ours.

If a boat had cruised our way on any average day out at sea, it would have found us bobbing quietly up and down over a long rolling swell covered with little white-crested waves, while the trade wind held the orange sail bent steadily toward Polynesia.

Those on board would have seen, at the stern of the raft, a brown bearded man with no clothes on, either struggling desperately with a long steering oar while he hauled on a tangled rope, or, in calm weather, just sitting on a box dozing in the hot sun and keeping a leisurely hold on the steering oar with his toes.

If this man happened not to be Bengt, then he would have been found lying on his stomach in the cabin door with one of his seventy-three sociological books. Bengt had further been appointed steward and was responsible for fixing the daily rations. Herman might

have been found anywhere at any time of the day—at the masthead with meteorological instruments, underneath the raft with diving goggles on checking a centerboard, or in tow in the rubber dinghy, busy with balloons and curious measuring apparatus.

Knut and Torstein were always doing something with their wet dry batteries, soldering irons, and circuits. All their wartime training was required to keep the little radio station going in spray and dew a foot above the surface of the water.

Every night they took turns sending our reports and weather observations out into the ether, where they were picked up by chance radio amateurs who passed the reports on to the Meteorological Institute in Washington and other destinations. Erik was usually sitting patching sails and splicing ropes, or carving in wood and drawing sketches of bearded men and odd fish. And at noon every day he took the sextant and mounted a box to look at the sun and find out how far we had moved since the day before. I myself had enough to do with the logbook and reports, the collecting of food from the sea, and taking pictures. Every man had his responsibility, and no one interfered with the others' work. All difficult jobs, like steering watch and cooking, were divided equally. Every man had two hours each day and two hours each night at the steering oar. And duty as cook was in accordance with a daily roster. There were few laws and regulations on board, except that the night watch must have a rope round his waist, that the life-saving rope had its regular place, that all meals were consumed outside the cabin wall, and that the toilet was at the farthest end of the logs astern. If an important decision was to be taken on board, we called a powwow in Indian style and discussed the matter together before anything was settled.

Knut and Torstein had to spend a part of each day working on the radio to keep it in repair.

Herman had charge of the meteorological instruments and he took the daily weather observations.

MEALS ON BOARD

An ordinary day on board the *Kon-Tiki* began with the last night watch shaking some life into the cook, who crawled out sleepily on to the dewy deck in the morning sun and began to gather flying fish. Instead of eating the fish raw, according to both Polynesian and Peruvian recipes, we fried them over a small primus stove at the bottom of a box which stood lashed fast to the deck outside the cabin door. This box was our kitchen. Here there was usually shelter from the southeast trade wind which regularly blew on to our other quarter. Only when the wind and sea juggled too much with the primus flame did it set fire to the wooden box, and once, when the cook had fallen asleep, the whole box became a mass of flames which spread to the very wall of the bamboo cabin. But the fire on the wall was quickly put out when the smoke poured into the hut, for, after all, we had never far to go for water on board the *Kon-Tiki*.

The smell of fried fish seldom managed to wake the snorers inside the bamboo cabin, so the cook usually had to stick a fork into them or sing "Breakfast's ready!" so out of tune that no one could bear to listen to him any longer. If there were no shark's fins alongside the raft, the day began with a quick plunge in the Pacific, followed by breakfast in the open air on the edge of the raft.

The food on board was divided into two experimental menus, one dedicated to the quartermaster and the twentieth century, one to Kon-Tiki and the fifth century. Torstein and Bengt were the subjects of the first experiment and restricted their diet to the slim little packages of special provisions which we had squeezed down into the hole between the logs and the bamboo deck. Every few weeks we untied the lashings which held down the bamboo deck and took out fresh supplies, which we lashed fast forward of the bamboo cabin. The tough layer of asphalt outside the cardboard proved resistant, while the hermetically sealed tins lying loose beside it were penetrated and ruined by the surrounding sea water.

Kon-Tiki, on his original voyage across the sea, had no asphalt or hermetically sealed tins; nevertheless he had no serious food problems. In those days, too, supplies consisted of what the men took with them from land and what they obtained for themselves on the voyage. We may assume that, when Kon-Tiki sailed from the coast of Peru after his defeat by Lake Titicaca, he had one of two objectives in mind. As the spiritual representative of the sun among a solely sun-worshiping people, it is

The provisions were stored between the logs and the deck. Our parrot always came fluttering along when we opened a box.

Breakfast on deck. We generally had our meals on the starboard side of the raft in front of the entrance to the cabin.

very probable that he ventured straight out to sea to follow the sun itself on its journey in the hope of finding a new and more peaceful country. An alternative possibility for him was to sail his rafts up the coast of South America in order to found a new kingdom out of reach of his persecutors. Clear of the dangerous rocky coast and hostile tribes along the shore, he would, like ourselves, fall an easy prey to the southeast trade wind and the Humboldt Current and, in the power of the elements, he would drift in exactly the same large semicircle right toward the sunset.

SWEET POTATOES AND GOURDS

Whatever these sun-worshipers' plans were when they fled from their homeland, they certainly provided themselves with supplies for the voyage. Dried meat and fish and sweet potatoes were the most important part of their primitive diet. When the raftsmen of that time put to sea along the desert coast of Peru, they had ample supplies of water on board. Instead of clay vessels they generally used the skin of giant bottle gourds, which was resistant to bumps and blows, while even more adapted to raft use were the thick canes of giant bamboos. They perforated through all the knots in the center and poured water in through a little hole at the end, which they stopped with a plug or with pitch or resin. Thirty or forty of these thick bamboo canes could be lashed fast along the raft under the bamboo deck, where they lay shaded and cool with fresh sea water—about 79° Fahrenheit in the Equatorial Current—washing about them. A store of this kind would contain twice as much water as we ourselves used on our whole voyage, and

71

still more could be taken by simply lashing on more bamboo canes in the water underneath the raft, where they weighed nothing and occupied no space.

We found that after two months fresh water began to grow stale and have a bad taste. But by then one is well through the first ocean area, in which there is little rain, and has arrived in regions where heavy rain showers can maintain the water supply. We served out a good quart of water per man daily, and it was by no means always that the ration was consumed.

Even if our predecessors had started from land with inadequate supplies, they would have managed well enough as long as they drifted across the sea with the current, in which fish abounded. There was not a day on our whole voyage on which fish were not swimming round the raft and could not easily be caught. Scarcely a day passed without flying fish, at any rate, coming on board of their own accord. It even happened that large bonitos, delicious eating, swam on board with the masses of water that came from astern and lay kicking on the raft when the water had vanished down between the logs as a sieve. To starve to death was impossible.

The old natives knew well the device which many shipwrecked men hit upon during the war—chewing thirst-quenching moisture out of raw fish. One can also press the juices out by twisting pieces of fish in a cloth, or, if the fish is large, it is a fairly simple matter to cut holes in its side, which soon become filled with ooze from the fish's lymphatic glands. It does not taste good if one has anything better to drink, but the percentage of salt is so low that one's thirst is quenched.

The necessity for drinking water was greatly reduced if we bathed regularly and lay down wet in the shady cabin. If a shark was patrolling majestically round about us and preventing a real plunge from the side of the raft, one had only to lie down on the logs aft and get a good grip of the ropes with one's fingers and toes. Then we got several bathfuls of crystal-clear Pacific pouring over us every few seconds.

We brought 275 gallons of fresh drinking water with us on the raft, and each man had a quart daily.

When tormented by thirst in a hot climate, one generally assumes that the body needs water, and this may often lead to immoderate inroads on the water ration without any benefit whatever. On really hot days in the tropics you can pour tepid water down your throat till you taste it at the back of your mouth, and you are just as thirsty. It is not liquid the body needs then, but, curiously enough, salt. The special rations we had on board included salt tablets to be taken regularly on particularly hot days, because perspiration drains the body of salt. We experienced days like this when the wind had died away and the sun blazed down on the raft without mercy. Our water ration could be ladled into us till it squelched in our stomachs, but our throats demanded much more. On such days we added from 20 to 40 per cent of bitter, salt sea water to our fresh-water ration and found, to our surprise, that this water quenched our thirst. We had the taste of sea water in our mouths for a long time afterward but never felt unwell, and, moreover, we had our water ration considerably increased.

One morning, as we sat at breakfast, an unexpected sea splashed into our gruel and taught us that the taste of oats removed the greater part of the sickening taste of sea water!

The old Polynesians had preserved some curious traditions, according to which their earliest forefathers, when they came sailing across the sea, had with them leaves of a certain plant which they chewed, with the result that their thirst disappeared. Another effect of the plant was that in an emergency they could drink sea water without being sick. No such plants grew in the South Sea islands; they must, therefore, have originated in their ancestors' homeland. The Polynesian historians repeated these statements so often that modern scientists investigated the matter and came to the conclusion that the only known plant with such an effect was the coca plant, which grew only in Peru.

We did not test coca leaves on board the *Kon-Tiki*, but we had on the foredeck large wicker baskets full of other plants, some of which had left a deeper imprint on the South Sea islands. The baskets stood lashed fast in the lee of the cabin wall, and as time passed yellow shoots and green leaves of potatoes and coconuts shot up higher and higher from the wickerwork. It was like a little tropical garden on board the wooden raft.

When the first Europeans came to the Pacific islands, they found large plantings of sweet potatoes on Easter Island and in Hawaii and New Zealand, and the same plant was also cultivated on the other islands, but only within the Polynesian area. It was quite unknown in the part of the world which lay farther west. The sweet potato was one of the most important cultivated plants in these remote islands where the people otherwise lived mainly on fish, and many of the Polynesians' legends centered round this plant. According to tradition it had been brought by no less a personage than Tiki himself, when he came with his wife Pani from their ancestors' original homeland, where the sweet potato had been an important article of food. New Zealand legends affirm that the sweet potato was brought over the sea in vessels which were not canoes but consisted of "wood bound together with ropes."

Now, as is known, America is the only place in the rest of the world where the potato grew before the time of Europeans. And the sweet potato Tiki brought with him to the islands is exactly the same as that which the Indians have cultivated in Peru from the oldest times. Dried sweet potatoes were the most important travel provisions both for the seafarers of Polynesia and for the natives in old Peru. In the South Sea islands the sweet potato will grow only if carefully tended by man, and, as it cannot withstand sea water, it cannot have floated by itself over 4,000 sea miles with ocean currents from Peru. This attempt to explain away so important a clue to the Polynesians' origin is particularly futile seeing that on all the widely scattered South Sea islands the name of the sweet potato is *kumara*, and *kumara* is just what the sweet potato was called among the old Indians in Peru. The name followed the plant across the sea.

Another very important Polynesian cultivated plant we had with us on board the *Kon-Tiki* was the bottle gourd. As important as the

The sweet potato and the bottle gourd are important links between Polynesia and Peru.

fruit itself was the skin, which the Polynesians dried over a fire and used to hold water. This typical garden plant also, which again cannot propagate itself in a wild state by drifting across the sea alone, the old Polynesians had in common with the original population of Peru. Bottle gourds, converted into water containers, are found in prehistoric desert graves on the coast of Peru and were used by the fishing population there centuries before men came to the Pacific islands.

COCONUTS AND CRABS

In addition to a few chance tropical fruits, most of which we ate up in a few weeks' time before they spoiled, we had on board a third plant which, along with the sweet potato, has played the greatest part in the history of Polynesia. We had two hundred coconuts, and they gave us exercise for our teeth and refreshing drinks. Several of the nuts soon began to sprout, and, when we had been just ten weeks at sea, we had half a dozen baby palms a foot high, which had already opened their shoots and formed thick green leaves. The coconut grew before Columbus' time both on the Isthmus of Panama and in South America. It was found in great numbers along the coast of Peru when the Spaniards arrived. At that time it had long existed on all the islands in the Pacific.

Botanists have still no certain proof in which direction it spread over the Pacific. But one thing has now been discovered. Not even the coconut, with its famous shell, can spread over the ocean without men's help. The nuts we had in baskets on deck remained eatable and capable of germinating the whole way to Polynesia. But we had laid about half among the special provisions below deck, with the waves washing around them. Every single one of these was ruined by the sea water. And no coconut can float over the sea faster than a balsa raft moves with the wind behind it. It

The seeds of the coconut palm may very well have been carried to Polynesia on rafts such as the *Kon-Tiki*.

was the eyes of the coconut, attacked by micro-organisms, that sucked in the sea water so that the nut spoiled. Refuse collectors, large and small, all over the ocean took care that no edible thing that floated should get across from one world to the other.

Solitary petrels and other sea birds which can sleep on the sea we met thousands of sea miles from the nearest land. Sometimes, on quiet days far out on the blue sea, we sailed close to a white, floating bird's feather. If, on approaching the little feather, we looked at it closely, we saw that there were two or three passengers on board it, sailing along at their ease before the wind. When the *Kon-Tiki* was about to pass, the passengers noticed that a vessel was coming which was faster and had more space, and so all came scuttling sideways at top speed over the surface and up on to the raft, leaving the feather to sail on alone. And so the *Kon-Tiki* soon began to swarm with stowaways. They were small pelagic crabs. As big as a fingernail, and now and then a good deal larger, they were tidbits for us if we managed to catch them.

The small crabs were the policemen of the sea's surface, and they were not slow to look after themselves when they saw anything eatable. If one day the cook failed to notice a flying fish in between the logs, next day it was covered with from eight to ten small crabs, sitting on the fish and helping themselves with their claws. Most often they were frightened and scurried away to hide when we came in view, but aft, in a little hole by the steering block, lived a crab that was quite tame and which we named Johannes.

Like the parrot, who was everyone's amusing pet, the crab Johannes became one of our community on deck. If the man at the helm, sitting steering on a sunshiny day with his back to the cabin, had not Johannes for company, he felt utterly lonely out on the wide blue sea. While the other small crabs scurried furtively about and pilfered like cockroaches on an ordinary boat, Johannes sat broad and round in his doorway with his eyes wide open, waiting for the change of watch. Every man who came on watch had a scrap of biscuit or a

The crab Johannes lived in a hole by the steering block and would eat from our fingers.

bit of fish for him, and we needed only to stoop down over the hole for him to come right out on his doorstep and stretch out his hands. He took the scraps out of our fingers with his claws and ran back into the hole, where he sat down in the doorway and munched like a schoolboy, cramming his food into his mouth.

The crabs clung like flies to the soaked coconuts, which burst when they fermented, or caught plankton, the tiniest organisms in the sea, when washed on board by the waves.

PLANKTON

Fish and sea birds which do not eat plankton themselves live on other fish or sea animals which do, no matter how large they themselves may be. Plankton is a general name for thousands of species of visible and invisible small organisms which drift about near the surface of the sea. Some are plants, while others are loose fish eggs and tiny living creatures. Animal plankton live on vegetable plankton, and vegetable plankton live on ammonia, nitrates, and nitrites which are formed from dead animal plankton. And while they live on one another, they all form food for everything which moves in and over the sea.

In good plankton waters there are thousands in a glassful. More than once persons have starved to death at sea because they did not find fish large enough to be spitted, netted, or hooked. In such cases it has often happened that they have literally been sailing about in

Plankton, the tiniest organisms in the sea, occur in an amazing and never-ending variety of shapes and colors.

strongly diluted, raw fish soup. If, in addition to hooks and nets, they had had a utensil for straining the soup they were sitting in, they would have found a nourishing meal—plankton. Some day in the future, perhaps, men will think of harvesting plankton from the sea to the same extent as now they harvest grain on land.

The marine biologist Dr. A. D. Bajkov told us of plankton and sent us a fishing net which was suited to the creatures we were to catch. The "net" was a silk net with almost three thousand meshes per square inch. It was sewn in the shape of a funnel with a circular mouth behind an iron ring, eighteen inches across, and was towed behind the raft. Just as in other kinds of fishing, the catch varied with time and place. Catches diminished as the sea grew warmer farther west, and we got the best results at night, because many species seemed to go deeper down into the water when the sun was shining.

If we had no other way of whiling away time on board the raft, there would have been entertainment enough in lying with our noses in the plankton net. Not for the sake of the smell, for that was bad. Nor because the sight was appetizing, for it looked a horrible mess. But because, if we spread the plankton out on a board and examined each of the little creatures separately with the naked eye, we had

before us fantastic shapes and colors in unending variety.

There was an endless variety of small creatures which might have been taken from Walt Disney's *Fantasia*. Some looked like fringed, fluttering spooks cut out of cellophane paper, while others resembled tiny red-beaked birds with hard shells instead of feathers. There was no end to Nature's extravagant inventions in the plankton world.

Where the cold Humboldt Current turned west south of the Equator, we could pour several pounds of plankton porridge out of the bag every few hours. The plankton lay packed together like cake in colored layers—brown, red, gray, and green according to the different fields of plankton through which we had passed. At night, when there was phosphorescence about, it was like hauling in a bag of sparkling jewels. But, when we got hold of it, the pirates' treasure turned into millions of tiny glittering shrimps and phosphorescent fish larvae that glowed in the dark like a heap of live coals. When we poured them into a bucket, the squashy mess ran out like a magic gruel composed of glowworms. Our night's catch looked as nasty at close quarters as it had been pretty at long range. And, bad as it smelled, it tasted correspondingly good if one just plucked up courage and put a spoonful of it into one's mouth. If this consisted of many dwarf shrimps, it tasted like shrimp paste, lobster, or crab. If it was mostly deep-sea fish eggs, it tasted like caviar and now and then like oysters.

The inedible vegetable plankton were either so small that they washed away with the water through the meshes of the net, or they were so large that we could pick them up with our fingers. "Snags" in the dish were two kinds of jellyfish. These were bitter and had to be thrown away. Otherwise everything could be eaten, either as it was or cooked in fresh water as gruel or soup. Tastes differ. Two men on board thought plankton tasted delicious, two thought they were quite good, and for two the sight of them was more than enough. From a nutrition standpoint they stand on a level with the larger shellfish, and, spiced and properly prepared, they can certainly be a first-class dish for all who like marine food.

That these small organisms contain calories enough has been proved by the blue whale, which is the largest animal in the world and yet lives on plankton. Our own method of capture, with the little net which was often chewed up by hungry fish, seemed to us sadly primitive when we sat on the raft and saw a passing whale send up cascades of water as it simply filtered plankton through its celluloid beard. And one day we lost the whole net in the sea.

WHALES, ANTS, AND BARNACLES

One day, when we were sitting as usual on the edge of the raft having a meal, so close to the water that we had only to lean back to wash out our mugs, we started when suddenly something behind us blew hard like a swimming horse and a big whale came up and stared at us, so close that we saw a shine like a polished shoe down through its blowhole. It was so unusual to hear real breathing out at sea, where all living creatures wriggle silently about without lungs and quiver their gills, that we really had a warm family feeling for our old distant cousin the whale, who like us had strayed so far out to sea. Instead of the cold, toadlike whale shark, which had not even the sense to stick up its nose for a breath of fresh air, here we had a visit from something which recalled a well-fed jovial hippopotamus in a zoological gardens and which actually breathed—that made a most pleasant impression on me—before it sank into the sea again and disappeared.

We were visited by whales many times. Most often they were small porpoises and toothed whales which gamboled about us in large schools on the surface of the water, but now and then there were big cachalots, too, and other giant whales which appeared singly or in small schools. Sometimes they passed like ships on the horizon, now and again sending a cascade of water into the air, but sometimes they steered straight for us. We were prepared for a dangerous collision the first time a big whale altered course and came straight toward the raft in a purposeful manner. As it gradually grew nearer, we could hear its blowing and puffing, heavy and long drawn, each time it rolled its head out of the water. It was an enormous, thick-skinned, ungainly land animal that came toiling through the water, as unlike a fish as a bat is unlike a bird. It came straight toward our port side, where we stood gathered on the edge of the raft, while one man sat at the masthead and shouted that he could see seven or eight more making their way toward us.

The big, shining, black forehead of the first whale was not more than two yards from us when it sank beneath the surface of the water, and then we saw the enormous blue-black bulk glide quietly under the raft right beneath our feet. It lay there for a time, dark and motionless, and we held our breath as we looked down on the gigantic curved back of a mammal a good deal longer than the whole raft. Then it sank slowly through the bluish water and disappeared from sight. Meanwhile the whole school were close upon us, but they paid no attention to us. Whales which have abused their giant strength and sunk whaling boats with their tails have presumably been attacked first. The whole morning we had them puffing and blowing round us in the most unexpected places without their even pushing against the raft or the steering oar. They quite enjoyed themselves gamboling freely among the waves in the sunshine. But about noon the whole school dived as if on a given signal and disappeared for good.

It was not only whales we could see under the raft. If we lifted up the reed matting we slept on, through the chinks between the logs we saw right down into the crystal-blue water. If we lay thus for a while, we saw a breast fin or tail fin waggle past and now and again we saw a whole fish. If the chinks had been a few inches wider, we could have lain comfortably in bed with a line and fished under our mattresses.

The fish which most of all attached themselves to the raft were dolphins and pilot fish. From the moment the first dolphins joined us in the current off Callao, there was not a day on the whole voyage on which we had not large dolphins wriggling round us. What drew them to the raft we do not know, but, either there was a magical attraction in being able to swim in the shade with a moving roof above them, or there was food to be found in our kitchen garden of seaweed and barnacles that hung like garlands from the logs and from the steering oar. It began with a thin coating of smooth green, but then the clusters of seaweed grew with astonishing speed, so that the *Kon-Tiki* looked like a bearded sea-god as she tumbled along among the waves. Inside the green seaweed was a favorite resort of tiny small fry and our stowaways, the crabs.

There was a time when ants began to get the upper hand on board. There had been small black ants in some of the logs, and, when we had got to sea and the damp began to penetrate into the wood, the ants swarmed out and into the sleeping bags. They were all over the place, and bit and tormented us till we thought they would drive us off the raft. But

Whales were frequent visitors. One day a whole school came puffing and blowing around us, even diving under the raft.

gradually, as it became wetter out at sea, they realized that this was not their right element, and only a few isolated specimens held out till we reached the other side. What did best on the raft, along with the crabs, were barnacles from an inch to an inch and a half long. They grew in hundreds, especially on the lee side of the raft, and as fast as we put the old ones into the soup kettle new larvae took root and grew up. The barnacles tasted fresh and delicate; we picked the seaweed as salad and it was eatable, though not so good. We never actually saw the dolphins feeding in the vegetable garden, but they were constantly turning their gleaming bellies upward and swimming under the logs.

DOLPHINS

The dolphin (dorado), which is a brilliantly colored tropical fish, must not be confused with the creature, also called dolphin, which is a small, toothed whale. The dolphin was ordinarily from three feet three inches to four feet six inches long and had much flattened sides with an enormously high head and neck. We jerked on board one which was four feet eight inches long with a head thirteen and one-half inches high. The dolphin had a magnificent color. In the water it shone blue and

Dolphins followed us throughout the voyage. They were beautiful to watch and also made excellent eating.

green like a bluebottle with a glitter of golden-yellow fins. But if we hauled one on board, we sometimes saw a strange sight. As the fish died, it gradually changed color and became silver gray with black spots and, finally, a quite uniform silvery white. This lasted for four or five minutes, and then the old colors slowly reappeared. Even in the water the dolphin could occasionally change color like a chameleon, and often we saw a "new kind" of shining copper-colored fish, which on a closer acquaintance proved to be our old companion the dolphin.

The high forehead gave the dolphin the appearance of a bulldog flattened from the side. When the dolphin was in a good humor,

79

it turned over on its flat side, went ahead at a great speed, and then sprang high into the air and tumbled down like a flat pancake. It came down on the surface with a regular smack and a column of water rose up. It was no sooner down in the water than it came up in another leap, and yet another, away over the swell. But, when it was in a bad temper—for example, when we hauled it up on the raft—then it bit. Torstein limped about for some time with a rag round his big toe because he had let it stray into the mouth of a dolphin, which had used the opportunity to close its jaws and chew a little harder than usual. After our return home we heard that dolphins attack and eat people when bathing. This was not very complimentary to us, seeing that we had bathed among them every day without their showing any particular interest.

Flying fish were the dolphins' favorite food. If anything splashed on the surface of the water, they rushed at it blindly in the hope of its being a flying fish. In many a drowsy morning hour, when we crept blinking out of the cabin, and, half alseep, dipped a toothbrush into the sea, we became wide-awake with a jump when a thirty-pound fish shot out like lightning from under the raft and nosed at the toothbrush in disappointment. And, when we were sitting quietly at breakfast on the edge

of the raft, a dolphin might jump up and make one of its most vigorous sideway splashes, so that the sea water ran down our backs and into our food.

One day, when we were sitting at dinner, Torstein made a reality of the tallest of fish stories. He suddenly laid down his fork and put his hand into the sea, and, before we knew what was happening, the water was boiling and a big dolphin came tumbling in among us. Torstein had caught hold of the tail end of a fishing line which came quietly gliding past, and on the other end hung a completely astonished dolphin which had broken Erik's line when he was fishing a few days before.

There was not a day on which we had not six or seven dolphins following us in circles round and under the raft. On bad days there might be only two or three, but, on the other hand, as many as thirty or forty might turn up the day after. As a rule it was enough to warn the cook twenty minutes in advance if we wanted fresh fish for dinner. Then he tied a line to a short bamboo stick and put half a flying fish on the hook. A dolphin was there in a flash, plowing the surface with its head as it chased the hook, with two or three more in its wake. It was a splendid fish to play and, when freshly caught, its flesh was firm and delicious to eat, like a mixture of cod and

A leaping dolphin in pursuit of a flying fish. We could always catch a dolphin with a flying fish as bait.

The underside of the raft resembled an undersea vegetable garden. Sharks and pilot fish often circled about there. Note remoras attached to the shark. (Inset: a barnacle).

salmon. It kept for two days, which was all we needed, for there were fish enough in the sea.

We became acquainted with pilot fish in another way. Sharks brought them and left them to be adopted by us after the sharks' death. We had not been long at sea before the first shark visited us. And sharks soon became an almost daily occurrence. Sometimes the shark just came swimming up to inspect the raft and went on in search of prey after circling round us once or twice. But most often the sharks took up a position in our wake just behind the steering oar, and there they lay without a sound, stealing from starboard to port and occasionally giving a leisurely wag of their tails to keep pace with the raft's placid advance. The blue-gray body of the shark always looked brownish in the sunlight just below the surface, and it moved up and down with the seas so that the dorsal fin always stuck up menacingly. If there was a high sea, the shark might be lifted up by the waves high above our own level, and we had a direct side view of the shark as in a glass case as it swam toward us in a dignified manner with its fussy retinue of small pilot fish ahead of its jaws. For a few seconds it looked as if both the shark and its striped companions would swim right on board, but then the raft would lean over gracefully to leeward, rise over the ridge of waves, and descend on the other side.

CATCHING SHARKS

To begin with, we had a great respect for sharks on account of their reputation and their alarming appearance. There was an unbridled strength in the streamlined body, consisting of one great bundle of steel muscles, and a heartless greed in the broad flat head with the small, green cat's eyes and the enormous jaws which could swallow footballs. When the man at the helm shouted, "Shark alongside to starboard" or, "Shark alongside to port," we used to come out in search of hand harpoons and gaffs and station ourselves along the edge of the raft. The shark usually glided round us with the dorsal fin close up to the logs. And our respect for the shark increased when we saw that the gaffs bent like spaghetti when we struck them against the sandpaper armor on the shark's back, while the spearheads of the hand harpoons were broken in the heat of the battle. All we gained by getting through the shark's skin and into the gristle or muscle was a hectic struggle, in which the water boiled round us till the shark broke loose and was

Nine sharks, two tunnies, and a lot of bonitos made up this day's catch. The flying fish and squids came aboard of their own accord.

off, while a little oil floated up and spread itself out over the surface.

To save our last harpoon head we fastened together a bunch of our largest fishhooks and hid them inside the carcass of a whole dolphin. We slung the bait overboard with a precautionary multiplication of steel lines fastened to a piece of our own life line. Slowly and surely the shark came, and, as it lifted its snout above the water, it opened its great crescent-shaped jaws with a jerk and let the whole dolphin slip in and down. And there it stuck. There was a struggle in which the shark lashed the water into foam, but we had a good grip on the rope and hauled the big fellow, despite its resistance, as far as the logs aft, where it lay awaiting what might come and only gaped as though to frighten us with its parallel rows of sawlike teeth. Here we profited by a sea to slide the shark up over the low end logs, slippery with seaweed, and, after casting a rope round the tail fin, we ran well out of the way till the war dance was over.

In the gristle of the first shark we caught this way we found our own harpoon head, and we thought at first that this was the reason for

the shark's comparatively small fighting spirit. But later we caught shark after shark by the same method, and every time it went just as easily. Even if the shark could jerk and tug and certainly was fearfully heavy to play, it became quite spiritless and tame and never made full use of its giant strength if we only managed to hold the line tight without letting the shark gain an inch in the tug of war. The sharks we got on board were usually from six to ten feet long, and there were blue sharks as well as brown sharks. The last-named had a skin outside the mass of muscles through which we could not drive a sharp knife unless we struck with our whole strength, and often not even then. The skin of the belly was as impenetrable as that of the back; the five gill clefts behind the head on each side were the only vulnerable point.

When we hauled in a shark, black slippery remora fish were usually fixed tight to its body. By means of an oval sucking disc on the top of the flat head, they were fastened so tight that we could not get them loose by pulling their tails. But they themselves could break loose and skip away to take hold at another

A blue shark with its conqueror. We often cleared the water of sharks to be on the safe side in case one of us fell overboard.

place in a second. If they grew tired of hanging tightly to the shark when their host gave no sign of returning to the sea, they leaped off and vanished down between the chinks in the raft to swim away and find themselves another shark. If the remora does not find a shark, it attaches itself to the skin of another fish for the time being. It is generally as long as the length of a finger up to a foot. We tried the natives' old trick which they sometimes use when they have been lucky enough to secure a live remora. They tie a line to its tail and let it swim away. It then tries to suck itself on to the first fish it sees and clings so tightly that a lucky fisherman may haul in both fishes by the remora's tail. We had no luck. Every single time we let a remora go with a line tied to its tail, it simply shot off and sucked itself fast to one of the logs of the raft, in the belief that it had found an extra fine big shark. And there it hung, however hard we tugged on the line. We gradually acquired a number of these small remoras which hung on and dangled obstinately among the shells on the side of the raft, traveling with us right across the Pacific.

But the remora was stupid and ugly and never became such an agreeable pet as its lively companion the pilot fish. The pilot fish is a small cigar-shaped fish with zebra strips, which swims rapidly in a shoal ahead of the shark's snout. It received its name because it was thought that it piloted its half-blind friend the shark about in the sea. In reality, it simply goes along with the shark, and, if it acts independently, it is only because it catches sight of food within its own range of vision. The pilot fish accompanied its lord and master to the last second. But, as it could not cling fast to the giant's skin, as the remora does, it was completely bewildered when its old master suddenly disappeared up into the air and did not come down again. Then the pilot fish scurried about in a distracted manner, searching wildly, but always came back and wriggled along astern of the raft, where the shark had vanished skyward. But as time passed and the shark did not come down again, they had to look round for a new lord and master. And none was nearer to hand than the *Kon-Tiki* herself.

If we let ourselves down over the side of the raft, with our heads down in the brilliantly clear water, we saw the raft as the belly of a sea monster, with the steering oar as its tail and the centerboards hanging down like blunt fins. In between them all the adopted pilot fish swam, side by side, and took no notice of the bubbling human head except that one or two of them darted swiftly aside and peered right up its nose, only to wriggle back again unperturbed and take their places in the ranks of eager swimmers.

Our pilot fish patrolled in two detachments; most of them swam between the centerboards, the others in a graceful fan formation ahead of the bow. Now and then they shot away from the raft to snap some edible trifle we passed, and after meals, when we washed our crockery in the water alongside, it was as if we had emptied a whole cigar case of striped pilot fish among the scraps. There was not a single scrap they did not examine, and, so long as it was not vegetable food, down it went. These queer little fish huddled under our protecting wings with such childlike confidence that we, like the shark, had a fatherly protective feeling toward them. They became the *Kon-Tiki's* marine pets, and it was taboo on board to lay hands on a pilot fish.

After a succession of victories the *Kon-Tiki* soon had a following of forty or fifty pilot fish, and many of them liked our quiet forward movement, and our daily scraps, so much that they followed us for thousands of miles over the sea.

But occasionally some were faithless. One day, when I was at the steering oar, I suddenly noticed that the sea was boiling to southward and saw an immense shoal of dolphins come shooting across the sea like silver torpedoes. They did not come as usual, splashing along comfortably on their flat sides; but came rushing at frantic speed more through the air than through the water. The blue swell was whipped into white foam in one single turmoil of splashing fugitives, and behind them came a black back dashing along on a zigzag course like a speedboat. The desperate dolphins came shooting through and over the surface right up to the raft; here they dived, while about a hundred crowded together in a tightly packed shoal and swung away to eastward, so that the whole sea astern was a glittering mass of colors. The gleaming back behind them half rose above the surface, dived in a graceful curve under the raft, and shot astern after the shoal of dolphins. It was a devilish big fellow of a blue shark that seemed to be nearly twenty feet long. When it disappeared, a number of our pilot fish had gone too. They had found a more exciting sea hero to go campaigning with.

THE SQUID

The marine creature against which the experts had begged us to be most on our guard was the squid, for it could get on board the raft. The National Geographic Society in Washington had shown us reports and dramatic magnesium photographs from an area in the Humboldt Current where monstrous squid had their favorite resort and came up on to the surface at night. They were so voracious that, if one of them fastened on to a piece of meat and remained on the hook, another came and began to eat its captured kinsman. They had arms which could make an end of a big shark and set ugly marks on great whales, and a devilish beak like an eagle's hidden among their tentacles. We were reminded that they lay floating in the darkness with phosphorescent eyes and that their arms were long enough to feel about in every small corner of the raft, if they did not care to come right on board. We did not at all like the prospect of feeling cold arms round our necks, dragging us out of our sleeping bags at night, and we provided ourselves with saberlike machete knives, one for each of us, in case we should wake to the embrace of fumbling tentacles. There was nothing which seemed more disagreeable to us when we started, especially as the marine experts in Peru got on to the same subject and showed us on the chart where the worst area was—right in the Humboldt Current itself.

For a long time we saw no sign of them, either on board or in the sea. But then one morning we had the first warning that they must be in those waters. When the sun rose, we found on board a baby squid the size of a cat. It had come up on deck unaided in the course of the night and now lay dead with its arms twined round the bamboo outside the cabin door. A thick, black, inky liquid was smeared over the bamboo deck and lay in a pool round the squid. We wrote a page or two in the logbook with cuttle-fish ink, which was like India ink, and then flung the baby overboard for the pleasure of the dolphins.

We saw in this minor incident a warning of larger night visitors. If the baby could clamber on board, its hungry parent could no doubt do the same. But the next incident completely bewildered us. One morning we found a single smaller young squid on the top of the roof of palm leaves. This puzzled us very much. It could not have climbed up there, as the only ink marks were smeared in a ring round it in the middle of the roof. Nor had it been dropped by a sea bird, for it was completely intact with no beak marks. We came to the conclusion that it had been flung up on to the roof by a sea which had come on board, but none of those on night watch could remember any such sea that night. As the nights passed, we regularly found more young squids on board, the smallest of them the size of one's middle finger.

It was soon usual to find one or two small ones among the flying fish about the deck in the morning, even if the sea had been calm in the night. And they were young ones of the real devilish kind, with eight long arms covered with sucking discs and two still longer with thornlike hooks at the end. But large squids never gave a sign of coming on board. We saw the shine of phosphorescent eyes drifting on the surface on dark nights, and on one single occasion we saw the sea boil and bubble while something like a big wheel came up and rotated in the air, while some of our dolphins tried to escape by hurling themselves desperately through space. But why the big ones never came on board, when the small ones were constant night visitors, was a riddle to which we found no answer until two months later after we were out of the ill-famed squid area.

Young squids continued to come aboard. One sunny morning we all saw a glittering shoal of something which shot up out of the water and flew through the air like large raindrops, while the sea boiled with pursuing dolphins.

The squid propels itself backward at high speed, its tentacles streaming behind it. Sometimes it shoots above the water like a flying fish.

phins. At first we took it for a shoal of flying fish, for we had already had three different kinds of these on board. But, when they came near and some of them sailed over the raft at a height of four or five feet, one ran straight into Bengt's chest and fell slap on the deck. It was a small squid. Our astonishment was great. When we put it into a sailcloth bucket it kept on taking off and shooting up to the surface, but it did not develop speed enough in the small bucket to get more than half out of the water.

It is a known fact that the squid ordinarily swims on the principle of the rocket propelled airplane. It pumps sea water with great force through a closed tube alongside its body and can thus shoot backward in jerks at a high speed; with all its tentacles hanging behind it in a cluster over its head it becomes streamlined like a fish. It has on its sides two round, fleshy folds of skin which are ordinarily used for steering and quiet swimming in the water. But our experience showed that defenseless young squids, which are a favorite food of

85

many large fish, can escape their pursuers by taking to the air in the same way as flying fish. They had made the principle of the rocket aircraft a reality long before human genius hit upon the idea. They pump sea water through themselves till they get up a terrific speed, and then they steer up at an angle from the surface by unfolding the pieces of skin like wings. Like the flying fish, they make a glider flight over the waves for as far as their speed can carry them. After that, when we had to begin to pay attention, we often saw them sailing along for fifty to sixty yards, singly and in two's and three's. The fact that squids can "glide" has been a novelty to all the zoologists we have met.

As the guest of natives in the Pacific I have often eaten squid; it tastes like a mixture of lobster and India rubber. But on board the *Kon-Tiki* squid came last on the menu. If we got them on deck free, we just exchanged them for something else. We made the exchange by throwing out a hook, with the squid on it, and pulling it in again with a big fish kicking at the end of it. Even tunny and bonito liked young squids.

But we did not run up against acquaintances only, as we lay drifting over the sea's surface. The diary contains many entries of this type:

—*11/5. Today a huge marine animal twice came up to the surface alongside us as we sat at supper on the edge of the raft. It made a fearful splashing and disappeared. We have no idea what it was.*

—*6/6. Herman saw a thick dark-colored fish with a broad white body, thin tail, and spikes. It jumped clear of the sea on the starboard side several times.*

—*16/6. Curious fish sighted on port bow. Six feet long, maximum breadth one foot; long, brown, thin snout, large dorsal fin near head and a smaller one in the middle of the back, heavy sickle-shaped tail fin. Kept near surface and swam at times by wriggling its body like an eel. It dived when Herman and I went out in the rubber dinghy with a hand harpoon. Came up later but dived again and disappeared.*

—*Next day: Erik was sitting at the masthead, 12 noon, when he saw thirty or forty long, thin, brown fish of the same kind as yesterday. Now they came at a high speed from the port side and disappeared astern like a big, brown, flat shadow in the sea.*

—*18/6. Knut observed a snakelike creature, two to three feet long and thin, which stood straight up and down in the water below the surface and dived by wriggling downward like a snake.*

On several occasions we glided past a large dark mass, the size of the floor of a room, that lay motionless under the surface of the water like a hidden reef. It was presumably the giant ray of evil repute but it never moved, and we never went close enough to make out its shape clearly.

With such company in the water time never passed slowly. It was even more entertaining when we had to dive down into the sea ourselves and inspect the ropes on the underside of the raft. One day one of the centerboards broke loose and slipped down under the raft, where it was caught up in the

Swimming under the raft was sometimes dangerous. Erik finally made a diving basket to give us some protection from inquisitive sharks.

ropes without our being able to get hold of it. Herman and Knut were the best divers. Twice Herman swam under the raft and lay there among dolphins and pilot fish, tugging and pulling at the board. He had just come up for the second time, and was sitting on the edge of the raft to recover his breath, when an eight-foot shark was detected not more than ten feet from his legs, moving steadily up from the depths toward the tips of his toes. Perhaps we did the shark an injustice, but we suspected it of evil intentions and rammed a harpoon into its skull. The shark felt aggrieved and a splashy struggle took place, as a consequence of which the shark disappeared leaving a sheet of oil on the surface, while the centerboard remained unsalved, lying caught up under the raft.

THE DIVING BASKET

Then Erik had the idea of making a diving basket. We had not many materials we could use, but we had bamboos and ropes and an old chip basket which had contained coconuts. We lengthened the basket upward with bamboos and plaited ropework, and then let one another down in the basket alongside the raft. Our enticing legs were then concealed in the basket, and, even if the plaited rope-work above had only a psychological effect on both us and the fish, in any case we could duck down into the basket in a flash if anything with hostile intentions made a dash at us, and have ourselves pulled up out of the water by the others on deck.

This diving basket was not merely useful but gradually became a perfect place of entertainment for all of us on board. It gave us a first-class opportunity to study the floating aquarium we had under the raft floor.

When the sea was content to run in a calm swell, we crawled into the basket one by one and were let down under water for as long as our breath lasted. There was a curiously transfigured, shadowless flow of light down in the water. As soon as we had our eyes under the surface, light and shadow no longer seemed to have a particular direction, as up in our own above-water world. If we looked up at the bottom of the raft, it was

Concealed in the diving basket, we could study the fascinating marine life under the raft at our ease.

brightly illuminated all over, with the nine big logs and the whole network of rope lashings bathed in a magic light and with a flickering wreath of spring-green seaweed all round the sides and along the whole length of the steering oar. The pilot fish swam formally in their ranks like zebras in fishes' skins, while big dolphins circled round with restless, vigilant, jerky movements, eager for prey. Here and there the light fell on the sappy red wood of a centerboard which stuck downward out of a chink, and on them sat peaceful colonies of white barnacles rhythmically beckoning for oxygen and food with their fringed yellow gills. If anyone came too near them, they hastily closed their red- and yellow-edged shells till they felt the danger was over.

The light down here was wonderfully clear and soothing for us who were accustomed to the tropical sun on deck. Even when we looked down into the bottomless depths of the sea, where it is eternal black night, the night appeared to us a brilliant light blue on account of the refracted rays of the sun. To our astonishment, we saw fish far down in the depths of the clear, clean blue when we ourselves were only just below the surface. They might have been bonitos, and there were other kinds which swam at such a depth that we could not recognize them. Sometimes they were in immense shoals, and we often wondered whether the whole ocean current was full of fish, or whether those down in the depths had intentionally assembled under the *Kon-Tiki* to keep us company for a few days.

What we liked best was a dip under the surface when the great gold-finned tunnies were paying us a visit. Occasionally they came to the raft in big shoals, but most often just two or three came together and swam round us in quiet circles for several days on end, unless we were able to lure them on to the hook. From the raft they looked simply like big, heavy, brown fish without any distinctive adornment, but if we crept down to them in their own element they spontaneously changed both color and shape. The change was so bewildering that several times we had to come up and take our bearings afresh to see if it was the same fish we had been looking at across the water. The big fellows paid no attention to us whatever—they continued their majestic maneuvers unperturbed—but now they had acquired a marvelous elegance of form, the equal of which we never saw in any other fish, and their color had become metallic with a suffusion of pale violet. Powerful torpedoes of shining silver and steel, with perfect proportions and streamlined shape, they had only to move one or two fins slightly to set their 150 to 200 pounds gliding about in the water with wonderful grace.

The closer we came into contact with the sea and what had its home there, the less strange it became and the more at home we ourselves felt.

A PHANTOM REEF

There were not many fixed marks out here at sea. Waves and fish, sun and stars, came and went. There was not supposed to be land of any sort in the 4,300 sea miles that separated the South Sea islands from Peru. We were therefore greatly surprised when we approached 100° west and discovered that a reef was marked on the Pacific chart right ahead of us on the course we were following. It was marked as a small circle, and, as the chart had been issued the same year, we looked up the reference in *Sailing Directions for South America*. We read that "breakers were reported in 1906 and again in 1926 to exist about 600 miles southwestward of Galapagos Islands, in latitude 6° 42′ S., longitude 99° 43′ W. In 1927 a steamer passed one mile westward of this position but saw no indication of breakers, and in 1934 another passed one mile southward and saw no evidence of breakers. The motor vessel 'Cowrie,' in 1935, obtained no bottom at 160 fathoms in this position."

According to the chart the place was clearly still regarded as a doubtful one for shipping, but, as a deep-draught vessel runs a greater risk by going too near a shoal than we should with a raft, we decided to steer straight for the point marked on the chart and see what we found. The reef was marked a little farther north than the point we seemed to be making for, so we laid the steering oar over to starboard and trimmed the square sail so that the bow pointed roughly north and we took sea and wind from the starboard side. Now it came about that a little more Pacific splashed into our sleeping bags than we were accustomed to, especially as at the same time the weather began to freshen considerably. But we saw to our satisfaction that the *Kon-Tiki* could be maneuvered surely and steadily at a surprisingly wide angle into the wind, so long as the wind was still on our quarter. Otherwise the sail swung round, and we had the same mad circus business to get the raft under control again.

Erik checking our position with the sextant as we drew near the position of the reported reef. No evidence of the reef was found.

For two days and nights we drove the raft north-northwest. The seas ran high and became incalculable as the trade wind began to fluctuate between southeast and east, but we were lifted up and down over all the waves that rushed against us. We had a constant lookout at the masthead, and when we rode over the ridges the horizon widened considerably. The crests of the seas reached six feet above the level of the roof of the bamboo cabin, and, if two vigorous seas rushed together, they rose still higher in combat and flung up a hissing watery tower which might burst down in unexpected directions. When night came, we barricaded the doorway with provision boxes, but it was a wet night's rest. We had hardly fallen asleep when the first crash on the bamboo wall came, and, while a thousand jets of water sprayed in like a fountain through the bamboo wickerwork, a foaming torrent rushed in over the provisions and on to us.

"Ring up the plumber," I heard a sleepy voice remark, as we hunched ourselves up to give the water room to run out through the floor. The plumber did not come, and we had a lot of bathwater in our beds that night. A big

dolphin actually came on board unintentionally in Herman's watch.

Next day the seas were less confused, as the trade wind had decided that it would now blow for a time from due east. We relieved one another at the masthead, for now we might expect to reach the point we were making for late in the afternoon. We noticed more life than usual in the sea that day. Perhaps it was only because we kept a better lookout than usual.

During the forenoon we saw a big swordfish approaching the raft close to the surface. The two sharp pointed fins which stuck up out of the water were six feet apart, and the sword looked almost as long as the body. The swordfish swept in a curve close by the man at the helm and disappeared behind the wave crests. When we were having a rather wet and salty midday meal, the carapace, head, and sprawling fins of a large sea turtle were lifted up by a hissing sea right in front of our noses. When that wave gave place to two others, the turtle was gone as suddenly as it had appeared. This time too we saw the gleaming whitish-green of dolphins' bellies tumbling about in the water below the armored reptile. The area was unusually rich in tiny flying fish an inch long, which sailed along in big shoals and often came on board. We also noted single skuas and were regularly visited by frigate birds, with forked tails like giant swallows, which cruised over the raft. Frigate birds are usually regarded as a sign that land is near, and the optimism on board increased.

"Perhaps there is a reef or a sandbank there all the same," some of us thought. And the most optimistic said: "Suppose we find a little green grassy island—one can never know since so few people have been here before. Then we'll have discovered a new land—Kon-Tiki Island!"

From noon onward Erik was more and more diligent in climbing up on the kitchen box and standing blinking through the sextant. At 6:20 P.M. he reported our position as latitude 6° 42′ south by longitude 99° 42′ west. We were 1 sea mile due east of the reef on the chart. The bamboo yard was lowered and the sail rolled up on deck. The wind was due east and would take us slowly right to the place. When the sun went down swiftly into the sea, the full moon in turn shone out in all its brilliance and lit up the surface of the sea, which undulated in black and silver from horizon to horizon. Visibility from the masthead was good. We saw breaking seas everywhere in long rows, but no regular surf which would indicate a reef or shoal. No one would turn in; all stood looking out eagerly, and two or three men were aloft at once.

As we drifted in over the center of the marked area, we sounded all the time. All the lead sinkers we had on board were fastened to the end of a fifty-four-thread silk rope more than 500 fathoms long, and, even if the rope hung rather aslant on account of the raft's leeway, at any rate the lead hung at a depth of some 400 fathoms. There was no bottom east of the place, or in the middle of it, or west of it. We took one last look over the surface of the sea, and, when we had assured ourselves that we could safely call the area surveyed and free from shallows of any kind, we set sail and laid the oar over in its usual place, so that

wind and sea were again on our port quarter.

And so we went on with the raft on her natural free course. The waves came and went as before between the open logs aft. We could now sleep and eat dry, even if the heaving seas round us took charge in earnest and raged for several days while the trade wind vacillated from east to southeast.

On this little sailing trip up to the spurious reef we had learned quite a lot about the effectiveness of the centerboards as a keel, and when, later in the voyage, Herman and Knut dived under the raft together and salved the fifth centerboard, we learned still more about these curious pieces of board, something which no one has understood since the Indians themselves gave up this forgotten sport. That the board did the work of a keel and allowed the raft to move at an angle to the wind—that was plain sailing. But when the old Spaniards declared that the Indians to a large extent "steered" their balsa rafts on the sea with "certain centerboards which they pushed down into the chinks between the timbers," this was hard to understand for us and for all who had concerned themselves with the problem. As the centerboard was simply held tight in a narrow chink, it could not be turned sideways and serve as a helm.

CENTERBOARD SOLVES A RIDDLE

We discovered the secret in the following manner: The wind was steady and the sea had gone down again, so that the *Kon-Tiki* had kept a steady course for a couple of days without our touching the lashed steering oar. We pushed the recovered centerboard down into a chink aft, and in a moment the *Kon-Tiki* altered course several degrees from west toward northwest and proceeded steadily and quietly on her new course. If we pulled this centerboard up again, the raft swung back on to her previous course. But if we pulled it only halfway up, the raft swung only halfway back on her old course. By simply raising and lowering the centerboards we could effect changes of course and keep to them without touching the steering oar.

This was the Incas' ingenious system. They

(A) Types of decorated center-boards used by the Peruvian Indians. (B) By raising or lowering the centerboards, the steersman could control the course of the raft without using a steering oar. (From *Juan and Ulloa*, 1748).

had worked out a simple system of balances by which pressure of the wind on the sail made the mast the fixed point. The two arms were the raft forward of and the raft aft of the mast. If the centerboard surface aft was heavier, the bow swung freely round with the wind; but if the centerboard surface forward was heavier, the stern swung round with the wind. The centerboards which are nearest the mast have, of course, the least effect on account of the relation between arm and power. If the wind was due astern, the centerboards ceased to be effective, and then it was impossible to keep the raft steady without continually working the steering oar. If the raft lay thus at full length, she was a little too long to ride the seas freely. As the cabin door and the place where we had meals were on the starboard side, we always took the seas on board on our port quarter.

We could certainly have continued our voyage by making the steersman stand and pull a centerboard up and down in a chink instead of hauling sidewise on the ropes of the steering oar, but we had now grown so accustomed to the steering oar that we just set a general course with the centerboards and preferred to steer with the oar.

The next great stage on our voyage was as invisible to the eye as the shoal which existed only on the map. It was the forty-fifth day at sea; we had advanced from the 78th degree of longitude to the 108th and were exactly halfway to the first islands ahead. There were over 2,000 sea miles between us and South America to the east, and it was the same distance on to Polynesia in the west. The nearest land in any direction was the Galapagos Islands to east-northeast and Easter Island due south, both more than 500 sea miles away on the boundless ocean. We had not seen a ship, and we never did see one, because we were off the routes of all ordinary shipping traffic in the Pacific.

But we did not really feel these enormous distances, for the horizon glided along with us unnoticed as we moved and our own floating world remained always the same—a circle flung up to the vault of the sky with the raft itself as center, while the same stars rolled on over us night after night.

Rowing in the dinghy was a pastime we all enjoyed in fair weather.

6. Across the Pacific

WHEN THE SEA was not too rough, we were often out in the little rubber dinghy taking photographs. I shall not forget the first time the sea was so calm that two men felt like putting the balloon-like little thing into the water and going for a row. They had hardly got clear of the raft when they dropped the little oars and sat roaring with laughter. And, as the swell lifted them away and they disappeared and reappeared among the seas, they laughed so loud every time they caught a glimpse of us that their voices rang out over the desolate Pacific. We looked around us with mixed feelings and saw nothing comic but our own bearded faces; but as the two in the dinghy should be accustomed to those by now, we began to have a lurking suspicion that they had suddenly gone mad. Sunstroke, perhaps. The two fellows could hardly scramble back on board the *Kon-Tiki* for sheer laughter and, gasping, with tears in their eyes they begged us just to go and see for ourselves.

Two of us jumped down into the dancing rubber dinghy and were caught by a sea which lifted us clear. Immediately we sat down with a bump and roared with laughter. We had to scramble back on the raft as quickly as possible and calm the last two who had not been out yet, for they thought we had all gone stark staring mad.

It was ourselves and our proud vessel that made such a completely hopeless, lunatic impression on us the first time we saw the whole thing at a distance. We had never before had an outside view of ourselves in the open sea. The logs of timber disappeared behind the smallest waves, and, when we saw anything at all, it was the low cabin with the wide doorway and the bristly roof of leaves that bobbed up from among the seas. The raft looked exactly like an old Norwegian hayloft lying helpless, drifting about in the open sea—a warped hayloft full of sunburned bearded ruffians. If anyone had come paddling after us at sea in a bathtub, we should have felt the same spontaneous urge to laughter. Even an ordinary swell rolled halfway up the cabin wall and looked as if it would pour in unhindered through the wide open door in which the bearded fellows lay gaping. But then the crazy craft came up to the surface again, and the vagabonds lay there as dry, shaggy, and intact as before. If a higher sea came racing by, cabin and sail and the whole mast might disappear behind the mountain of water, but just as certainly the cabin with its vagabonds would be there again next moment. The situation looked bad, and we could not realize that things had gone so well on board the zany craft.

A NEAR DISASTER

Next time we rowed out to have a good laugh at ourselves we nearly had a disaster. The wind and sea were higher than we supposed, and the *Kon-Tiki* was cleaving a path for herself over the swell much more quickly than we realized. We in the dinghy had to row for our lives out in the open sea in an attempt to regain the unmanageable raft, which could not stop and wait and could not possibly turn around and come back. Even when the boys on board the *Kon-Tiki* got the sail down, the wind got such a grip on the bamboo cabin that the raft drifted away to westward as fast as we could splash after her in the dancing rubber dinghy with its tiny toy oars. There was only one thought in the head of every man—we must not be separated. Those were horrible minutes we spent out on the sea before we got hold of the runaway raft and crawled on board to the others, home again.

From that day it was strictly forbidden to go out in the rubber dinghy without having a long line made fast to the bow, so that those who remained on board could haul the dinghy in if necessary. We never went far away from the raft, thereafter, except when the wind was light and the Pacific curving itself in a gentle swell. But we had these conditions when the raft was halfway to Polynesia and the ocean, all dominating, arched itself round the globe toward every point of the compass. Then we could safely leave the *Kon-Tiki* and row away into the blue space between sky and sea.

When we saw the silhouette of our craft grow smaller and smaller in the distance, and the big sail at last shrunken to a vague black square on the horizon, a sensation of loneliness sometimes crept over us. The sea curved away under us as blue upon blue as the sky above, and where they met all the blue flowed together and became one. It almost seemed as if we were suspended in space. All our world was empty and blue; there was no fixed point in it but the tropical sun, golden and warm, which burned our necks. Then the distant sail of the lonely raft drew us to it like a magnetic point on the horizon. We rowed back and crept on board with a feeling that we had come home again to our own world—on board and yet on firm, safe ground. And inside the bamboo cabin we found shade and the scent of bamboo and withered palm leaves. The sunny blue purity outside was now served to us in a suitably large dose through the open cabin wall. So we were accustomed to it and so it was good for a time, till the great clear blue tempted us out again.

THE BAMBOO HUT

It was most remarkable what a psychological effect the shaky bamboo cabin had on our minds. It measured eight by fourteen feet, and to diminish the pressure of wind and sea it was built low so that we could not stand upright under the ridge of the roof. Walls and roof were made of strong bamboo canes, lashed together and guyed, and covered with a tough wickerwork of split bamboos. The green and yellow bars, with fringes of foliage hanging down from the roof, were restful to the eye as a white cabin wall never could have been, and, despite the fact that the bamboo wall on the starboard side was open for one third of its length and roof and walls let in sun and moon, this primitive lair gave us a greater feeling of security than white-painted bulkheads and closed portholes would have given in the same circumstances.

The fact that the balsa logs always rode the seas like a gull, and let the water right through aft if a wave broke on board, gave us an unshakable confidence in the dry part in the middle of the raft where the cabin was. The longer the voyage lasted, the safer we felt in our cozy lair, and we looked at the white-crested waves that danced past outside our doorway as if they were an impressive movie, conveying no menace to us at all. Even though the gaping wall was only five feet from the unprotected edge of the raft and only a foot and a half above the water line, yet we felt as if we had traveled many miles away from the sea and occupied a jungle dwelling remote from the sea's perils once we had crawled inside the door. There we could lie on our backs and look up at the curious roof which twisted about like boughs in the wind, enjoying the jungle smell of raw wood, bamboos, and withered palm leaves.

Sometimes, too, we went out in the rubber boat to look at ourselves by night. Coal-black seas towered up on all sides, and a glittering myriad of tropical stars drew a faint reflection from plankton in the water.

Before us in the night the *Kon-Tiki* rose out of the seas to sink down again behind black masses of water that towered between her and us. In the moonlight there was a fantastic atmosphere about the raft. Stout, shining wooden logs fringed with seaweed, the

When we felt musical, Erik was always ready to accompany our singing with his guitar.

Inside the bamboo cabin we were protected against both wind and tropical sun. From left: Herman, Knut, Erik, Bengt, the author.

square pitch-black outline of a Viking sail, a bristly bamboo hut with the yellow light of a paraffin lamp aft—the whole suggested a picture from a fairytale rather than an actual reality. Now and then the raft disappeared completely behind the black seas; then she rose again and stood out sharp in silhouette against the stars, while glittering water poured from the logs.

When we jumped on board the raft again, we often sat down in a circle round the paraffin lamp on the bamboo deck and talked of the seafarers from Peru who had had all these same experiences fifteen hundred years before us. The lamp flung huge shadows of bearded men on the sail, and we thought of the white men with the beards from Peru whom we could follow in mythology and architecture all the way from Mexico to Central America and into the northwestern area of South America as far as Peru. Here this mysterious civilization disappeared, as by the stroke of a magic wand, before the coming of the Incas and reappeared just as suddenly out on the solitary Pacific islands which we were now approaching.

THE MYSTERY OF EASTER ISLAND

It is the island nearest to Peru, Easter Island, which bears the deepest traces of civilization. This insignificant little island, dry and barren, is the farthest from Asia of all the islands in the Pacific.

When we had completed half our voyage, we had sailed just the distance from Peru to Easter Island and had the legendary island due south of us. We had left land at a chance point in the middle of the coast of Peru to imitate an average raft putting to sea. If we had left the land farther south, nearer Kon-Tiki's ruined city Tiahuanaco, we should have got the same wind but a weaker current, both of which would have carried us in the direction of Easter Island.

When we passed 110° west, we were within the Polynesian ocean area, inasmuch as the Polynesian Easter Island was now nearer Peru

95

than we were. We were on a line with the first outpost of the South Sea islands, the center of the oldest island civilization. And when at night our glowing road guide, the sun, climbed down from the sky and disappeared beyond the sea in the west with his whole spectrum of colors, the gentle trade wind blew life into the stories of the strange mystery of Easter Island. While the night sky smothered all concept of time, we sat and talked and bearded giants' heads were again thrown upon the sail.

Easter Island is the top of an extinct submarine volcano. Paved roads laid down by the old civilized inhabitants lead to well-preserved landing places on the coast and show that the water level round the island was exactly the same then as it is today. This is no remains of a sunken continent but a tiny desolate island, which was as small and solitary when it was a vivid cultural center as it is today.

Near the eastern corner of this triangular island lies one of the extinct craters, and here lies the sculptors' amazing quarry and workshop. It lies there exactly as the old artists and architects left it hundreds of years ago, when they fled in haste to the eastern extremity of the island where, according to tradition, all but one were slain and burned in a ditch in a battle which made the present Polynesians victors and rulers of the island. According to Easter Island tradition, the defeated artists, "the long-ears," had white skin, red hair, and spoke a foreign language. The sudden interruption of the artists' work gives a clear cross section of an ordinary working day in the Easter Island crater wall. The sculptors' stone tools, hard as flint, lie strewn about their working places and show that this advanced people was as ignorant of iron as Kon-Tiki's sculptors were when they were driven in flight from Peru, leaving behind them other gigantic stone statues on the Andes plateau. In both places the quarries can be found where legendary white people hewed statues and building blocks of stone thirty feet long or more right out of the mountainside with the help of tools of still harder stone. And in both places the gigantic statues and blocks, weighing tens of tons, were transported for many miles over rough ground before being set up on end as enormous human figures, or placed on top of one another to form temple terraces and walls.

THE STONE GIANTS

Many huge unfinished figures still lie where they were begun, in their niches in the crater wall on Easter Island, and show how the work was carried on in different stages. The largest human figure, which was almost completed when the builders had to flee, was sixty-nine feet long; if it had been finished and set up, the head would have been level with the top of an seven-floor building. Every separate figure was hewn out of a single connected block of stone, and the working niches for sculptors round the lying stone figures show that not many men were at work at the same time on each figure. Lying on their backs with their arms bent and their hands placed on their stomachs, exactly like the stone statues in South America, the Easter Island figures were completed in every minute detail before they were removed from the workshop and transported to their destinations round about on the island. In the last stage inside the quarry the giant was attached to the cliff side by only a narrow ridge under his back; then this too was hewn away, the giant meanwhile being supported by boulders.

Large quantities of these figures were just dragged down and raised in the slopes inside and outside the crater. But a number of the largest were transported up and over the wall of the crater, and for many miles round over difficult country, before being set up on a stone platform and having an extra stone cylinder of red tuff placed on their heads. This transport in itself may appear to be a complete mystery, but we cannot deny that it took place or that the architects who disappeared from Peru left in the Andes Mountains stone statues of equal size, which show that they too were experts in this very line.

The sculptors' work in the quarry took a long time but required only a few experts. The work of transport each time a statue was completed was more quickly done but, on the other hand, required large numbers of men.

Easter Island
(RAPA NUI)

0 1 2
Miles

An old print showing one of the statues with topknot still in place.

With primitive stone tools, the ancient sculptors carved the giant statues in the walls of an extinct crater. When a statue was completed it was hauled over the wall of the crater and set upright.

A partially excavated statue, showing the rainbow belt, the traditional emblem of the sun-god.

Little Easter Island was then both rich in fish and thoroughly cultivated, with large plantations of Peruvian sweet potatoes, and it is believed that the island in its great days could have supported a population of seven or eight thousand. About a thousand men were quite enough to haul huge statues even up and over the steep crater wall, while five hundred were sufficient to drag them on farther across the island.

Solid cables were plaited from bast and vegetable fibers, and, using wooden sledges, the multitude dragged the stone statue along. That old civilized peoples were masters in making ropes and cables is well known from the South Sea islands and still more from Peru, where the first European found suspension bridges a hundred yards long laid across torrents and gorges by means of plaited cables as thick as a man's waist.

When the statue had arrived at its chosen site and was to be set up on end, the next prob-

lem arose. Now it had to be lifted up on a tall temple platform and raised on end. And not until then did the giant receive an enormous block of red stone to balance on top of its head.

But why did they make these statues? And why was it necessary to go off to another quarry four miles away from the crater workshop to find a special kind of red stone to place on the figure's head?

Let us see first whom the statues represented. When the first Europeans visited the island, they saw mysterious "white men" on shore, and some of them had red hair and beards. These were of the descendants of women and a single man spared during the massacre of the first race on the island. The natives themselves declared that one branch of their ancestors had been white, the other brown. They calculated precisely that the last had immigrated from elsewhere in Polynesia twenty-two generations before, while the first had come from the east in large vessels as much as fifty-seven generations back (*i.e.*, about 400–500 A.D.). The race which came from the east were given the name "long-ears," because they lengthened their ears artificially by hanging weights on the lobes so that they hung down to their shoulders. It was the mysterious "long-ears" who were killed when the Polynesian "short-ears" came to the island, and therefore all the stone figures on Easter Island had large ears hanging down to their shoulders, as the sculptors themselves had had.

Now the Inca legends in Peru say that the sun-king Kon-Tiki ruled over a white people with beards who were called by the Incas "big-ears," because they too had their ears artificially lengthened so that they reached down to their shoulders. The Incas emphasized that it was Kon-Tiki's "big-ears" who had erected the giant statues in the Andes Mountains before they were killed or driven out by the Incas themselves in the battle on an island in Lake Titicaca.

To sum up: Kon-Tiki's white "big-ears" disappeared from Peru *westward* with ample experience of working on colossal stone statues, and Tiki's white "long-ears" came to

Easter Island from *eastward* skilled in exactly the same art, which they at once took up in full perfection so that not the smallest trace can be found on Easter Island of any development leading up to the masterpieces on the island.

Although the Inca had black, straight hair, red-haired mummies with wavy hair are often found in the oldest Peruvian tombs. At the time of the European explorations there existed in Peru and on all the islands in Polynesia scattered individuals and whole families with reddish hair and fair skins, and the natives both in Peru and Polynesia declared that it was these who were descended from the first white people in their lands. On certain islands religious festivals were held, the participators in which colored their skins white and their hair red to resemble their earliest ancestors. At annual ceremonies on Easter Island the chief person of the festival had all his hair cut off so that his head might be painted red. And the colossal red-stone caps on the giant statues on Easter Island were called "top-knots" by the natives. They were also carved in the shape which was typical of the local hair style; they had a round knot on the top, just as the men had their hair tied in a little traditional topknot in the middle of the head.

The statues on Easter Island had long ears because the sculptors themselves had lengthened ears. They had specially chosen red stone wigs because the sculptors themselves had reddish hair. They had their chins carved pointed and projecting, because the sculptors themselves grew beards. They had the typical appearance of the white race with a straight and narrow nose and thin sharp lips, because the sculptors themselves did not belong to the Malay race. And when the statues had their hands laid in a strange position on their stomachs, it was because it was just in this way the people were accustomed to carve statues in South America. The sole decoration of the Easter Island figures is a belt which was always carved round the figure's stomach. The same symbolic belt is found on every single statue in Kon-Tiki's ancient ruins by Lake Titicaca. It is the legendary emblem of the sun-god, the rainbow belt. There was a myth on the island of Mangareva according to which the sun-god had taken off the rainbow which was his magic belt and climbed down it from the sky on to Mangareva to people the island with his white-skinned children. The sun was once regarded as the oldest original ancestor in some of these islands, as well as in Peru.

We used to sit on deck under the starry sky and retell Easter Island's strange history, even though our own raft was carrying us straight past far to the north of it and into the heart of Polynesia.

CATCHING SHARKS

We no longer had the same respect for waves and sea. We knew them and their relationship to us on the raft. Even the shark had become a part of the everyday picture; we knew it and its usual reactions. We no longer thought of the hand harpoon, and we did not even move away from the side of the raft, if a shark came up alongside. On the contrary, we were more likely to try and grasp its back fin as it glided unperturbed along the logs. This finally developed into a quite new form of sport—tug of war with shark without a line.

We began quite modestly. We caught all too easily more dolphins than we could eat. To keep a popular form of amusement going without wasting food, we hit on comic fishing without a hook for the mutual entertainment of the dolphins and ourselves. We fastened unused flying fish to a string and drew them over the surface of the water. The dolphins shot up to the surface and seized the fish, and then we tugged, each in our own direction, and had a fine circus performance, for if one dolphin let go another came in its place. We had fun, and the dolphins got the fish in the end.

Then we started the same game with the sharks. We had either a bit of fish on the end of a rope or often a bag with scraps from dinner, which we let out on a line. Instead of turning on its back, the shark pushed its snout above the water and swam forward with jaws wide to swallow the morsel. We could not help pulling on the rope just as the shark was

A hungry shark eating out of the author's hand.

Just as it is about to dive, the author seizes its tail fin.

Without the use of its tail, th shark can only struggle briefly.

going to close its jaws again, and the cheated animal swam on with an unspeakably foolish, patient expression and opened its jaws again for the offal, which jumped out of its mouth every time it tried to swallow it. It ended by the shark's coming right up to the logs and jumping up like a begging dog for the food which hung dangling in a bag above its nose. One day at the end of July the following entry was made in the diary:

—*We made friends with the shark which followed us today. At dinner we fed it with scraps which we poured right down into its open jaws. It has the effect of a half fierce, half good-natured and friendly dog when it swims alongside us. It cannot be denied that sharks can seem quite pleasant so long as we do not get into their jaws ourselves. At least we find it amusing to have them about us, except when we are bathing.*

One day a bamboo stick, with a bag of shark's food tied to a string, was lying ready for use on the edge of the raft when a sea came and washed it overboard. The bamboo stick was already lying afloat a couple of hundred yards astern of the raft, when it suddenly rose upright in the water and came rushing after the raft by itself, as if it intended to put itself nicely back in its place again. When the fishing rod came swaying nearer us, we saw a ten-foot shark swimming right under it, while the bamboo stick stuck up out of the waves like a periscope. The shark had swallowed the food

bag without biting off the line. The fishing rod soon overtook us, and vanished ahead.

But, even if we gradually came to look upon the shark with quite other eyes, our respect for the five or six rows of razor-sharp teeth which lay in ambush in the huge jaws never disappeared.

One day Knut had an involuntary swim in company with a shark. No one was ever allowed to swim away from the raft, both on account of the raft's drift and because of sharks. But one day it was extra quiet and we had just pulled on board such sharks as had been following us, so permission was given for a quick dip in the sea. Knut plunged in and had gone quite a long way before he came up to the surface to crawl back. At that moment we saw from the mast a shadow bigger than himself coming up behind him, deeper down. We shouted warnings as quietly as we could so as not to create a panic, and Knut heaved himself toward the side of the raft. But the shadow below belonged to a still better swimmer, which shot up from the depths and gained on Knut. They reached the raft at the same time. While Knut was clambering on board, a six-foot shark glided past right under his stomach and stopped beside the raft. We gave it a dainty dolphin's head to thank it for not having snapped.

Generally it is smell more than sight which excites the shark's appetite. We have sat with our legs in the water to test them, and they

When it becomes quiet, the shark is slowly hauled on deck.

One strong jerk and it is on board, where its struggles end.

have swum toward us till they were two or three feet away, only quietly to turn their tails toward us again. But, if the water was in the least bloodstained, as it was when we had been cleaning fish, the sharks' fins came to life and they would suddenly collect like bluebottles from a long way off. If we flung out shark's guts, they simply went mad and dashed about in a blind frenzy. They savagely devoured the liver of their own kind and then, if we put a foot into the sea, they came for it like rockets and even dug their teeth into the logs where the foot had been. The mood of a shark may vary immensely, the animal being completely at the mercy of its own emotions.

The last stage in our encounter with sharks was that we began to pull their tails. Pulling animals' tails is held to be an inferior form of sport, but that may be because no one has tried it on a shark. For it was, in truth, a lively form of sport.

To get hold of a shark by the tail we first had to give it a real tidbit. It was ready to stick its head high out of the water to get it. Usually it had its food served dangling in a bag. For, if one has fed a shark directly by hand once, it is no longer amusing. If one feeds dogs or tame bears by hand, they set their teeth into the meat and tear and worry it till they get a bit off or until they get the whole piece for themselves. But, if one holds out a large dolphin at a safe distance from the shark's head, the shark comes up and smacks his jaws to-

gether, and, without one's having felt the slightest tug, half the dolphin is suddenly gone and one is left sitting with a tail in one's hand. We had found it a hard job to cut the dolphin in two with knives, but in a fraction of a second the shark, moving its triangular saw teeth quickly sideways, had chopped off the backbone and everything else like a sausage machine.

When the shark turned quietly to go under again, its tail flickered up above the surface and was easy to grasp. The shark's skin was just like sandpaper to hold on to, and inside the upper point of its tail there was an indentation which might have been made solely to allow of a good grip. If we once got a firm grasp there, there was no chance of our grip not holding. Then we had to give a jerk, before the shark could collect itself, and get as

101

much as possible of the tail pulled in tight over the logs. For a second or two the shark realized nothing, but then it began to wriggle and struggle in a spiritless manner with the fore part of its body, for without the help of its tail a shark cannot get up any speed. The other fins are only for balancing and steering. After a few desperate jerks, during which we had to keep a tight hold of the tail, the surprised shark became quite crestfallen and apathetic, and, as the loose stomach began to sink down toward the head, the shark at last became completely paralyzed.

When the shark had become quiet and, as it were, hung stiff awaiting developments, it was time for us to haul in with all our might. We seldom got more than half the heavy fish up out of the water; then the shark too woke up and did the rest itself. With violent jerks it swung its head round and up on to the logs, and then we had to tug with all our might and jump well out of the way, and that pretty quickly, if we wanted to save our legs. For now the shark was in no kindly mood. Jerking itself round in great leaps, it thrashed at the bamboo wall, using its tail as a sledge hammer. Now it no longer spared its iron muscles. The huge jaws were opened wide, and the rows of teeth bit and snapped in the air for anything they could reach. It might happen that the war dance ended in the shark's more or less involuntarily tumbling overboard and disappearing for good after its shameful humiliation, but most often the shark flung itself about at random on the logs aft, till we got a running noose round the root of its tail or till it had ceased to gnash its devilish teeth forever.

THE PARROT

The parrot was quite thrilled when we had a shark on deck. It came scurrying out of the bamboo cabin and climbed up the wall at frantic speed till it found itself a good, safe lookout post on the palm-leaf roof, and there it sat shaking its head or fluttered to and fro along the ridge, shrieking with excitement. It had at an early date become an excellent sailor and was always bubbling over with humor and laughter. We reckoned ourselves as seven on board—six of us and the green parrot. The crab Johannes didn't really count. At night the parrot crept into its cage under the roof of the bamboo cabin, but in the daytime it strutted about the deck or hung on to guy ropes and stays and did the most fascinating acrobatic exercises.

At the start of the voyage we had turnbuckles on the stays of the mast but they wore the ropes, so we replaced them by ordinary running knots. When the stays stretched and grew slack from sun and wind, all hands had to turn to and brace up the mast, so that its mangrove wood, as heavy as iron, should not bump against and cut into the ropes till they fell down. While we were hauling and pulling, at the most critical moment the parrot began to call out with its cracked voice: "Haul! Haul! Ho, ho, ho, ho, ha ha ha!" And if it made us laugh, it laughed till it shook at its own cleverness and swung round and round on the stays.

At first the parrot was the bane of our radio operators. They might be sitting happily absorbed in the radio corner with their magic earphones on and perhaps in contact with a radio "ham" in Oklahoma. Then their earphones would suddenly go dead, and they could not get a sound however much they coaxed the wires and turned the knobs. The parrot had been busy and bitten off the wire of the aerial. This was specially tempting in the early days, when the wire was sent up with a little balloon. But one day the parrot became seriously ill. It sat in its cage and moped and touched no food for two days, while its droppings glittered with golden scraps of aerial. Then the radio operators repented of their angry words and the parrot of its misdeeds, and from that day Torstein and Knut were its chosen friends and the parrot would never sleep anywhere but in the radio corner. The parrot's mother tongue was Spanish when it first came on board; Bengt declared it took to talking Spanish with a Norwegian accent long before it began to imitate Torstein's favorite ejaculations in full-blooded Norwegian.

We enjoyed the parrot's humor and brilliant colors for two months, till a big sea came

Heave ho! The ropes became slack in tropical sun and squalls, and we often had to make them taut. The parrot enjoyed watching us.

on board from astern while it was on its way down the stay from the masthead. When we discovered that the parrot had gone overboard, it was too late. We did not see it. And the *Kon-Tiki* could not be turned or stopped; if anything went overboard from the raft, we had no chance of turning back for it—numerous experiences had shown that.

The loss of the parrot had a depressing effect on our spirits the first evening; we knew that exactly the same thing would happen to ourselves if we fell overboard on a solitary night watch. We tightened up on all the safety

regulations, brought into use new life lines for the night watch, and frightened one another out of believing that we were safe because things had gone well in the first two months. One careless step, one thoughtless movement, could send us where the green parrot had gone, even in broad daylight.

We had several times observed the large white shells of cuttlefish eggs, lying floating like ostrich eggs or white skulls on the blue swell. On one solitary occasion we saw a squid lying wriggling underneath. We observed the snow-white balls floating on a level with ourselves and thought at first it would be an easy matter to row out in the dinghy and get them. We thought the same that time when the rope of the plankton net broke so that the cloth net was left behind alone, floating in our wake. Each time we launched the dinghy, with a rope attached, to row back and pick up the floating object. But we saw to our surprise that the wind and sea held the dinghy off and that the line from the *Kon-Tiki* had so violent a braking effect in the water that we could never row right back to a point we had already left. We might get within a few yards of what we wanted to pick up, but then the whole line was out and the *Kon-Tiki* was pulling us away westward. "Once overboard always overboard" was a lesson that was gradually burned into our minds. If we wanted to go with the rest, we must hang on till the *Kon-Tiki* ran her bow against land on the other side.

The parrot left a blank in the radio corner, but, when the tropical sun shone out over the Pacific next day, we soon became reconciled to his loss. We hauled in many sharks the next few days, and we constantly found black curved parrots' beaks, or so we thought, among tunnies' heads and other curiosities in the shark's belly. But on closer examination the black beaks always proved to belong to squids.

The two radio operators had had a tough job in their corner since the first day they came on board. The very first day, in the

The radio station was a corner of the cabin blocked off by a cardboard partition.

Humboldt Current, sea water trickled even from the battery cases so that they had to cover the sensitive radio corner with canvas to save what could be saved in the high seas. And then they had the problem of fitting a long enough aerial on the little raft. They tried to send the aerial up with a kite, but in a gust of wind the kite simply plunged down into a wave crest and disappeared. Then they tried to send it up with a balloon, but the tropical sun burned holes in the balloon so that it collapsed and sank into the sea. And then they had the trouble with the parrot. In addition to all this, we were a fortnight in the Humboldt Current before we came out of a dead zone of the Andes in which the short wave was as dumb and lifeless as the air in an empty soapbox.

CONVERSATION BY SHORT WAVE

But then one night the short wave suddenly broke through, and Torstein's call signal was heard by a chance radio amateur in Los Angeles who was sitting fiddling with his transmitter to establish contact with another amateur in Sweden. The man asked what kind of set we had and, when he got a satisfactory answer to his question, he asked Torstein who he was and where he lived. When he heard that Torstein's abode was a bamboo cabin on a raft in the Pacific, there were several peculiar clickings until Torstein supplied more details. When the man on the air had pulled himself together, he told us that his name was Hal and his wife's name Anna and that she was Swedish by birth and would let our families know we were alive and well.

It was a strange thought for us that evening that a total stranger called Hal, a chance moving-picture operator far away among the swarming population of Los Angeles, was the only person in the world but ourselves who knew where we were and that we were well. From that night onward Hal, alias Harold Kempel, and his friend Frank Cuevas took it in turns to sit up every night and listen for signals from the raft, and Herman received grateful telegrams from the head of the U.S. Weather Bureau for his two daily code reports

We once established radio contact with Oslo, at the opposite end of the globe.

Knut and the parrot could wriggle their way about in that corner unscathed, and we put up a sheet of cardboard to mark the danger zone for the rest of us.

Late one night Knut was sitting tinkering by lamplight in the radio corner when he suddenly shook me by the leg and said he had been talking to a fellow who lived just outside Oslo and was called Christian Amundsen. This was a bit of an amateur record, for the little short-wave transmitter on board the raft with its 13,990 kilocycles per second did not send out more than 6 watts, about the same strength as a small electric torch. This was August 2, and we had sailed more than sixty degrees round the earth, so that Oslo was at the opposite end of the globe. King Haakon was seventy-five years old the day after, and we sent him a message of congratulations direct from the raft; the day after that Christian was again audible and sent us a reply from the King, wishing us continued good luck and success on our voyage.

Another episode we remember as an unusual contrast to the rest of the life on the raft. We had two cameras on board, and Erik had with him a parcel of materials for developing photographs on the voyage, so that we could take duplicate snapshots of things that had not come out well. After the whale shark's visit he could contain himself no longer, and one evening he mixed the chemicals and water carefully in exact accordance with the instructions and developed two films. The negatives looked like long-distance photographs—nothing but obscure spots and wrinkles. The film was ruined. We telegraphed to our contacts for advice, but our message was picked up by a radio amateur near Hollywood. He telephoned a laboratory and soon afterward he broke in and told us that our developer was too warm; we must not use water above 60° or the negative would be wrinkled.

We thanked him for his advice and found out that the very lowest temperature in our surroundings was that of the ocean current itself, which was nearly 80°. Now Herman was a refrigerating engineer, and I told him by way of a joke to get the temperature of the

from an area for which there were extremely few reports and no statistics. Later Knut and Torstein established contact with other radio amateurs almost every night, and these passed on greetings to Norway through a radio "ham" named Egil Berg at Notodden.

When we were just a few days out in mid-ocean, there was too much salt water for the radio corner, and the station stopped working altogether. The operators stood on their heads day and night with screws and soldering irons, and all our distant radio fans thought the raft's days were ended. But then one night the signals LI 2 B burst out into the ether, and in a moment the radio corner was buzzing like a wasp's nest as several hundred American operators seized their keys simultaneously and replied to the call.

Indeed one always felt as if one were sitting down on a wasp's nest if one strayed into the radio operators' domain. It was damp with sea water, which forced its way up along the woodwork everywhere, and, even if there was a piece of raw rubber on the balsa log where the operator sat, one got electric shocks both in the hinder parts and in the finger tips if one touched the Morse key. And, if one of us outsiders tried to steal a pencil from the well-equipped corner, either his hair stood straight up on his head or he drew long sparks from the stump of the pencil. Only Torstein and

The old Polynesians explored vast areas of the Pacific Ocean in rafts or double canoes, navigating by the stars.

water down to 60°. He asked to have the use of the little bottle of carbonic acid belonging to the already inflated rubber dinghy, and after some hocus-pocus in a kettle covered with a sleeping bag and a woolen vest suddenly there was snow on Herman's stubbly beard, and he came in with a big lump of white ice in the kettle.

Erik developed afresh with splendid results.

Even though the ghost words carried through the air by short wave were an unknown luxury in Kon-Tiki's early days, the long ocean waves beneath us were the same as of old and they carried the balsa raft steadily westward as they did then, fifteen hundred years ago.

The weather became a little more unsettled, with scattered rain squalls, after we had entered the area nearer the South Sea islands and the trade wind had changed its direction. It had blown steadily and surely from the southeast until we were a good way over in the Equatorial Current; then it had veered round more and more toward due east. We reached our most northerly position on June 10 with latitude 6° 19′ south. We were then so close up to the Equator that it looked as if we should sail above even the most northerly islands of the Marquesas group and disappear completely in the sea without finding land. But then the trade wind swung round farther, from east to northeast, and drove us in a curve down toward the latitude of the world of islands.

It often happened that wind and sea remained unchanged for days on end, and then we clean forgot whose steering watch it was except at night, when the watch was alone on deck. For, if sea and wind were steady, the steering oar was lashed fast and the Kon-Tiki sail remained filled without our attending to it. Then the night watch could sit quietly in the cabin door and look at the stars. If the constellations changed their position in the sky, it was time for him to go out and see whether it was the steering oar or the wind that had shifted.

STEERING BY THE STARS

It was incredible how easy it was to steer by the stars when we had seen them marching across the vault of the sky for weeks on end. Indeed, there was not much else to look at at night. We knew where we could expect to see the different constellations night after night, and, when we came up toward the Equator, The Great Bear rose so clear of the horizon in the north that we were anxious lest we should catch a glimpse of the Pole Star, which appears when one comes from southward and crosses the Equator. But as the northeasterly trade wind set in, the Great Bear sank again.

The old Polynesians were great navigators. They took bearings by the sun by day and the stars by night. Their knowledge of the heavenly bodies was astonishing. They knew that the earth was round, and they had their own names for such ideas as the Equator and the northern and southern tropics. In Hawaii they cut charts of the ocean on the shells of round bottle gourds, and on certain other islands they made detailed maps of plaited boughs to which shells were attached to mark the islands, while the twigs marked particular currents. The Polynesians knew five planets, which they called wandering stars, and distinguished them from the fixed stars, for which they had nearly two hundred different names. A good navigator in old Polynesia knew well in what part of the sky the different stars would rise and where they would be at different times of the night and at different times times of the year.

Apart from the fact that the starry sky lay like a glittering giant compass revolving from east to west, they understood that the different stars right over their heads always showed them how far north or south they were. When the Polynesians had explored and brought under their sway their present domain, which is the whole of the sea nearest to America, they maintained traffic between some of the islands for many generations to come. Historical traditions relate that, when the chiefs from Tahiti visited Hawaii, which lay more than 2,000 sea miles farther north and several degrees farther west, the helmsman steered first due north by sun and stars, till the stars right above their heads told them that they were on the latitude of Hawaii. Then they turned at a right angle and steered due west till they came so near that birds and clouds told them where the group of islands lay.

Whence had the Polynesians obtained their vast astronomical knowledge and their calendar, which was calculated with astonishing thoroughness? Certainly not from Melanesian or Malayan peoples to the westward. But the same old vanished civilized race, the "white and bearded men," who had taught Aztecs, Mayas, and Incas their amazing culture in America, had evolved a curiously similar calendar and a similar astronomical knowledge which Europe in those times could not match. In Polynesia, precisely as in Peru, the calendar year had been so arranged as to begin on the particular day of the year when the constellation of the Pleiades first appeared above the horizon, and in both areas this constellation was considered the patron of agriculture.

In Peru, where the continent slopes down toward the Pacific, are to this day in the desert sand the large remains of an astronomical observatory of great antiquity, a relic of the same mysterious civilized people which carved huge stone statues, erected pyramids, cultivated sweet potatoes and bottle gourds, and began their year with the rising of the Pleiades. Kon-Tiki knew the movement of the stars when he set sail upon the Pacific Ocean.

A STORM

On July 2 our night watch could no longer sit in peace studying the night sky. We had a strong wind and nasty sea after several days of light northeasterly breeze. Late in the night we had brilliant moonlight and a quite fresh sailing wind. We measured our speed by counting the seconds we took to pass a chip, flung out ahead on one side of us, and found that we were establishing a speed record. While our average speed was from twelve to eighteen "chips," in the jargon current on board, we were now for a time down to "six chips," and the phosphorescence swirled in a regular wake astern of the raft.

Four men lay snoring in the bamboo cabin while Torstein sat clicking with the Morse key and I was on steering watch. Just before midnight I caught sight of a quite unusual sea which came breaking astern of us right across the whole of my disturbed field of vision. Behind it I could see here and there the foaming crests of two more huge seas like the first, following hard on its heels. If we ourselves had not just passed the place, I should have been convinced that what I saw was high surf flung up over a dangerous shoal. I gave a warning shout as the first sea came like a long wall sweeping after us in the moonlight, and wrenched the raft into position to take what was coming.

When the first sea reached us, the raft flung her stern up sideways and rose up over the wave back which had just broken, so that it hissed and boiled all along the crest. We rode through the welter of boiling foam which poured along both sides of the raft, while the heavy sea itself rolled by under us. The bow flung itself up last as the wave passed, and we slid, stern first, down into a broad trough of the waves. Immediately after, the next wall of water came on and rose up, while we were again lifted hurriedly into the air and the clear water masses broke over us aft as we shot over the edge. As a result the raft was flung right broadside on to the seas, and it was impossible to wrench her round quickly enough.

The next sea came on and rose out of the stripes of foam like a glittering wall which began to fall along its upper edge just as it reached us. When it plunged down, I saw nothing else to do but hang on as tight as I could to a projecting bamboo pole of the cabin roof; there I held my breath while I felt that we were flung sky-high and everything round me carried away in roaring whirlpools of foam. In a second we and the *Kon-Tiki* were above water again and gliding quietly down a gentle wave back on the other side. Then the seas were normal again. The three great wave walls raced on before us, and astern in the moonlight a string of coconuts lay bobbing in the water.

The last wave had given the cabin a violent blow, so that Torstein was flung head over heels into the radio corner and the others woke, scared by the noise, while the water gushed up between the logs and in through the wall. On the port side of the foredeck the bamboo wickerwork was blown open like a small crater, and the diving basket had been knocked flat up in the bow, but everything else was as it had been. Where the three big seas came from, we have never been able to explain with certainty, unless they were due to

disturbances on the sea bottom, which are not so uncommon in these regions.

Two days later we had our first storm. It started by the trade wind dying away completely, and the feathery, white tradewind clouds, which were drifting over our heads up in the topmost blue, being suddenly invaded by a thick black cloud bank which rolled up over the horizon from southward. Then there came gusts of wind from the most unexpected directions, so that it was impossible for the steering watch to keep control. As quickly as we got our stern turned to the new direction of the wind, so that the sail bellied out stiff and safe, just as quickly the gusts came at us from another quarter, squeezed the proud bulge out of the sail, and made it swing round and thrash about to the peril of both crew and cargo. But then the wind suddenly set in to blow straight from the quarter whence the bad weather came, and, as the black clouds rolled over us, the breeze increased to a fresh wind which worked itself up into a real storm.

In the course of an incredibly short time the seas round about us were flung up to a height of fifteen feet, while single crests were hissing twenty and twenty-five feet above the trough of the sea, so that we had them on a level with our masthead when we ourselves were down in the trough. All hands had to scramble about on deck bent double, while the wind shook the bamboo wall and whistled and howled in all the rigging.

To protect the radio corner we stretched canvas over the rear wall and port side of the cabin. All loose cargo was lashed securely, and the sail was hauled down and made fast around the bamboo yard. When the sky clouded over, the sea grew dark and threatening, and in every direction it was whitecrested with breaking waves. Long tracks of dead foam lay like stripes to windward down the backs of the long seas; and everywhere, where

The waves towered about us and the wind howled, but the raft rode the seas easily.

the wave ridges had broken and plunged down, green patches like wounds lay frothing for a long time in the blue-black sea. The crests blew away as they broke, and the spray stood like salt rain over the sea. When the tropical rain poured over us in horizontal squalls and whipped the surface of the sea, invisible all round us, the water that ran from our hair and beards tasted salty, while we crawled about the deck naked and frozen, seeing that all the gear was in order to weather the storm.

When the storm rushed up over the horizon and gathered about us for the first time, strained anticipation and anxiety were discernible in our looks. But when it was upon us in earnest, and the *Kon-Tiki* took everything that came her way with ease and bouyancy, the storm became an exciting form of sport, and we all delighted in the fury round about us which the balsa raft mastered so easily, always seeing that she herself lay on the wave tops like a cork, while all the main weight of the raging water was always a few inches beneath. The sea had much in common with the mountains in such weather. It was like being out in the wilds in a storm, up on the highest mountain plateaus, naked and gray. Even though we were right in the heart of the tropics, when the raft glided up and down over the smoking waste of sea we always thought of racing downhill among snowdrifts and rock faces.

The steering watch had to keep its eyes open in such weather. When the steepest seas passed under the forward half of the raft, the logs aft rose right out of the water, but the next second they plunged down again to climb up over the next crest. Each time the seas came so close upon one another that the hindmost reached us while the first was still holding the bow in the air. Then the solid sheets of water thundered in over the steering watch in a terrifying welter, but next second the stern went up and the flood disappeared as through the prongs of a fork.

We calculated that in an ordinary calm sea, where there were usually seven seconds between the highest waves, we took in about two hundred tons of water astern in twenty-four

When the waves came close together, the helmsman had to hold hard to the steering oar to keep from being washed overboard.

hours. But we hardly noticed it because it just flowed in quietly round the bare legs of the steering watch and as quietly disappeared again between the logs. But in a heavy storm more than ten thousand tons of water poured on board astern in the course of twenty-four hours, seeing that loads varying from a few gallons to two or three cubic yards, and occasionally much more, flowed on board every five seconds. It sometimes broke on board with a deafening thunderclap, so that the helmsman stood in water up to his waist and felt as if he were forcing his way against the current in a swift river. The raft seemed to stand trembling for a moment, but then the cruel load that weighed her down astern disappeared overboard again in great cascades.

Herman was out all the time measuring the squalls of gale force, which lasted for twenty-four hours. Then they gradually dropped to a stiff breeze with scattered rain squalls, which continued to keep the seas boiling round us as we tumbled on westward with a good sailing wind. To obtain accurate wind measurements down among the towering seas Herman had, whenever possible, to make his way up to the swaying masthead, where it was all he could do to hold on.

FISH IN THE STORM

When the weather moderated, it was as though the big fish around us had become completely infuriated. The water round the raft was full of sharks, tunnies, dolphins, and a few dazed bonitos, all wriggling about close under the timber of the raft and in the waves nearest to it. It was a ceaseless life-and-death struggle; the backs of big fishes arched themselves over the water and shot off like rockets, one chasing another in pairs, while the water round the raft was repeatedly tinged with thick blood. The combatants were mainly tunnies and dolphins, and the dolphins came in big shoals which moved much more quickly and alertly than usual. The tunnies were the assailants; often a fish of 150 to 200 pounds would leap high into the air holding a dolphin's bloody head in its mouth. But, even if individual dolphins dashed off with tunnies hard on their heels, the actual shoal of dolphins did not give ground, although there were often several wriggling round with big gaping wounds in their necks. Now and again the sharks, too, seemed to become blind with rage, and we saw them catch and fight with big tunnies, which met in the shark a superior enemy.

Not one single peaceful little pilot fish was to be seen. They had been devoured by the furious tunnies, or they had hidden in the chinks under the raft or fled far away from the battlefield. We dared not put our heads down into the water to see.

I had a nasty shock—and could not help laughing afterward at my own complete bewilderment—when I was aft, obeying a call of nature. We were accustomed to a bit of a swell in the water closet, but it seemed contrary to all reasonable probabilities when I quite unexpectedly received a violent punch astern from something large and cold and very heavy, which came butting up against me like a shark's head in the sea. I was actually on my way up the mast stay, with a feeling that I had a shark hanging on to my hindquarters, before I collected myself. Herman, who was hanging over the steering oar doubled up with laughter, was able to tell me that a huge tunny had delivered a sideways smack at my nakedness with his 160 pounds or so of cold fish. Afterward, when Herman and then Torstein were on watch, the same fish tried to jump on board with the seas from astern, and twice the big fellow was right up on the end of the logs, but each time it flung itself overboard again before we could get a grip of the slippery body.

After that a stout bewildered bonito came right on board with a sea, and with that, and a tunny caught the day before, we decided to fish, to bring order into the hungry chaos that surrounded us. Our diary says:

—*A six-foot shark was hooked first and hauled on board. As soon as the hook was out again, it was swallowed by an eight-foot shark, and we hauled that on board. When the hook came out again, we got a fresh six-foot shark and had hauled it over the edge of the raft when it broke loose and dived. The hook went out again at once, and an eight-foot shark came on to it and gave us a hard tussle. We had its head over the logs when all four steel lines were cut through and the shark dived into the depths. New hook out, and a seven-foot shark was hauled on board. It was now dangerous to stand on the slippery logs aft fishing, because the three sharks kept on throwing up their heads and snapping, long after one would have thought they were dead. We dragged the sharks forward by the tail into a heap on the foredeck, and soon afterward a big tunny was hooked and gave us more of a fight than any shark before we got it on board. It was so fat and heavy that none of us could lift it by the tail.*

The sea was just as full of furious fish backs. Another shark was hooked but broke away just when it was being pulled on board. But then we got a six-foot shark safely on board. After that a five-foot shark, which also came on board. Then we caught yet another six-foot shark and hauled it up. When the hook came out again, we hauled in a seven-foot shark.

Wherever we walked on deck, there were big sharks lying in the way, beating their tails convulsively on the deck or thrashing against the bamboo cabin as they snapped around them. Already tired and worn out when we began to fish after the storm, we became completely befuddled as to which sharks were quite dead, which were still snapping convulsively if we went near them, and which were quite alive and were lying in ambush for us with their green cat's eyes. When we had nine big sharks lying round us in every direction, we were so weary of hauling on heavy lines and fighting with the twisting and snapping giants that we gave up after five hours' toil.

Next day there were fewer dolphins and tunnies but just as many sharks. We began to fish and haul them in again but soon stopped when we perceived that all the fresh shark's blood that ran off the raft only attracted still more sharks. We threw all the dead sharks overboard and washed the whole deck clean of blood. The bamboo mats were torn by shark teeth and rough sharkskin, and we threw the bloodiest and most torn of them overboard and replaced them with new golden-yellow bamboo mats, several layers of which were lashed fast on the foredeck.

When we turned in on these evenings, in our mind's eye we saw greedy, open shark jaws and blood. And the smell of shark meat stuck in our nostrils. We could eat shark—it tasted like haddock if we got the ammonia out of the pieces by putting them in sea water for twenty-four hours—but bonito and tunny were much better.

That evening, for the first time, I heard one of the fellows say that it would soon be pleasant to be able to stretch oneself out comfortably on the green grass on a palm island; he would be glad to see something other than cold fish and rough sea.

The weather had become quite quiet again, but it was never as constant and dependable as before. Incalculable, violent gusts of wind from time to time brought with them heavy showers, which we were glad to see because a large part of our water supply had begun to go bad and tasted like evil-smelling marsh water. When it was pouring the hardest, we collected water from the cabin roof and stood on deck naked, thoroughly to enjoy the luxury of having the salt washed off with fresh water.

The pilot fish were wriggling along again in their usual places, but whether they were the same old ones which had returned after the blood bath, or whether they were new followers taken over in the heat of the battle, we could not say.

On July 21 the wind suddenly died away again. It was oppressive and absolutely still, and we knew from previous experience what this might mean. And, right enough, after a few violent gusts from east and west and south, the wind freshened up to a breeze from southward, where black, threatening clouds had again rushed up over the horizon. Herman was out with his anemometer all the time, measuring already fifty feet and more per second, when suddenly Torstein's sleeping bag went overboard. And what happened in the next few seconds took a much shorter time than it takes to tell it.

MAN OVERBOARD

Herman tried to catch the bag as it went, took a rash step, and fell overboard. We heard a faint cry for help amid the noise of the waves, and saw Herman's head and a waving arm as well as some vague green object twirling about in the water near him. He was struggling to get back to the raft through the high seas which had lifted him out from the port side. Torstein, who was at the steering oar aft, and I myself, up in the bow, were the first to perceive him, and we went cold with fear. We bellowed "Man overboard!" at the top of our lungs as we rushed to the nearest life-saving gear. The others had not heard Herman's cry because of the noise of the sea, but in a trice there was life and bustle on deck. Herman was an excellent swimmer, and, though we realized at once that his life was at stake, we had a fair hope that he would manage to crawl back to the edge of the raft before it was too late.

Torstein, who was nearest, seized the bamboo drum round which was the line we used for the lifeboat, for this was within his reach. It was the only time on the whole voyage that this line got caught up. Herman was now on a level with the stern of the raft but a few yards away, and his last hope was to crawl to the blade of the steering oar and hang on to it. As he missed the end of the logs, he reached out for the oar blade, but it slipped away from him. And there he lay, just where experience had shown we could get nothing back. While Bengt and I launched the dinghy, Knut and Erik threw out the life belt. Carrying a long line, it hung ready for use on the corner of the cabin roof, but today the wind was so strong that when it was thrown it was simply blown back to the raft. After a few unsuccessful throws Herman was already far astern of the steering oar, swimming desperately to keep up with the raft, while the distance increased with each gust of wind. He realized that henceforth the gap would simply go on increasing, but he set a faint hope on the dinghy which we had now got into the water. Without the line, which acted as a brake, it would perhaps be possible to drive the rubber raft to meet the swimming man, but whether the rubber raft would ever get back to the *Kon-Tiki* was another matter. Nevertheless, three men in a rubber dinghy had some chance; one man in the sea had none.

Then we suddenly saw Knut take off and plunge headfirst into the sea. He had the life belt in one hand and was heaving himself along. Every time Herman's head appeared on a wave back Knut was gone, and every time Knut came up Herman was not there. But then we saw both heads at once; they had swum to meet each other and both were hanging on to the life belt. Knut waved his arm, and, as the rubber raft had meanwhile been hauled on board, all four of us took hold of the line of the life belt and hauled for dear life, with our eyes fixed on the great dark object which was visible just behind the two men. This same mysterious beast in the water was pushing a big greenish-black triangle up above the wave crests; it almost gave Knut a shock when he was on his way over to Herman. Only Herman knew then that the triangle did not belong to a shark or any other sea monster. It was an inflated corner of Torstein's watertight sleeping bag. But the sleeping bag did not remain floating for long after we had hauled the two men safe and sound on board.

Man overboard! Only quick action could save Herman before he was left far astern, for the raft could not be stopped or turned back.

Whatever dragged the sleeping bag down into the depths had just missed a better prey.

"Glad I wasn't in it," said Torstein and took hold of the steering oar where he had let it go.

But otherwise there were not many wisecracks that evening. We all felt a chill running through nerve and bone for a long time afterward. But the cold shivers were mingled with a warm thankfulness that there were still six of us on board.

We had a lot of nice things to say to Knut that day—Herman and the rest of us, too.

But there was not much time to think about what had already happened, for as the sky grew black over our heads the gusts of wind increased in strength, and before night a new storm was upon us. We finally got the life belt to hang astern of the raft on a long line, so that we had something behind the steering oar toward which to swim if one of us should fall overboard again in a squall. Then it grew pitch dark around us as night fell and hid the raft and the sea. Bouncing wildly up and down in the darkness, we only heard and felt the gale howling in masts and guy ropes, while the gusts pressed with smashing force against the springy bamboo cabin till we thought it would fly overboard. But it was covered with canvas and well guyed. And we felt the *Kon-Tiki* tossing with the foaming seas, while the logs moved up and down with the movement of the waves like the keys of an instrument. We were astonished that cascades of water did not gush up through the wide chinks in the floor, but they only acted as a regular bellows through which damp air rushed up and down.

THE KON-TIKI WEAKENS

For five whole days the weather varied between full storm and light gale; the sea was dug up into wide valleys filled with the smoke from foaming gray-blue seas, which seemed to have their backs pressed out long and flat under the onset of the wind. Then on the fifth day the heavens split to show a glimpse of blue, and the malignant, black cloud cover gave place to the ever victorious blue sky as the storm passed on. We had come through

the gale with the steering oar smashed and the sail rent; the centerboards hung loose and banged about like crowbars among the logs, because all the ropes which had tightened them up under water were worn through. But we ourselves and the cargo were completely undamaged.

After the two storms the *Kon-Tiki* had become a good deal weaker in the joints. The strain of working over the steep wave backs had stretched all the ropes, and the continuously working logs had made the ropes eat into the balsa wood. We thanked Providence that we had followed the Incas' custom and had not used wire ropes, which would simply have sawed the whole raft into matchwood in the gale. And, if we had used bone-dry, high-floating balsa at the start, the raft would long ago have sunk into the sea under us, saturated with sea water. It was the sap in the fresh logs which prevented the water from filtering in through the porous balsa wood.

But now the ropes had become so loose that it was dangerous to let one's foot slip down between two logs, for it could be crushed when they came together violently. Forward and aft, where there was no bamboo deck, we had to give at the knees when we stood with our feet wide apart on two logs at the same time. The logs aft were as slippery as banana leaves with wet seaweed, and, even though we had made a regular path through the greenery where we usually walked and had laid down a broad plank for the steering watch to stand on, it was not easy to keep one's foothold when a sea struck the raft. On the port side one of the nine giants bumped and banged against the crossbeams with dull, wet thuds both by night and by day. There came also new and fearful creakings from the ropes which held the two sloping masts together at the masthead, for the steps of the masts worked about independently of each other, because they rested on two different logs.

We got the steering oar spliced and lashed with long billets of mangrove wood, as hard as iron, and with Erik and Bengt as sailmakers Kon-Tiki soon raised his head again and swelled his breast in a stiff bulge toward Polynesia, while the steering oar danced behind in seas which the fine weather had made soft and gentle. But the centerboards never again became quite what they had been; they did not meet the pressure of the water with their full strength but gave way and hung, dangling loose and unguyed, under the raft. It was useless to try to inspect the ropes on the underside, for they were completely overgrown with seaweed. On taking up the whole bamboo deck we found only three of the main ropes broken; they had been lying crooked and pressed against the cargo, which had worn them away. It was evident that the logs had absorbed a great weight of water but, since the cargo had been lightened, this was roughly canceled out. Most of our provisions and drinking water were already used up, likewise the radio operators' dry batteries.

Nevertheless, after the last storm it was clear enough that we should both float and hold together for the short distance that separated us from the islands ahead. Now quite another problem came into the foreground—how would the voyage end?

The *Kon-Tiki* would slog on ever westward until she ran her bow into a solid rock or some other fixed object which would stop her drifting. But our voyage would not be ended until all hands had landed safe and sound on one of the numerous Polynesian islands ahead.

When we came through the last storm, it was quite uncertain where the raft would end up. We were at an equal distance from the Marquesas Islands and the Tuamotu group, and in a position which meant that we could very easily pass right between the two groups of islands without having a glimpse of one of them. The nearest island in the Marquesas group lay 300 sea miles northwest, and the nearest island in the Tuamotu group lay 300 sea miles southwest, while wind and current were uncertain, with their general direction westerly and toward the wide ocean gap between the two island groups.

The island which lay nearest to the northwest was no other than Fatu Hiva, the little jungle-clad mountainous island where I had

Repairing the steering oar after the storm. Although the *Kon-Tiki* had weakened, it was still seaworthy.

lived in a hut built on piles on the beach and heard the old man's vivid stories of the ancestral hero Tiki. If the *Kon-Tiki* stood in to that same beach, I should meet many acquaintances, but hardly the old man himself. He must have departed long ago. If the raft headed in toward the mountain ranges of the Marquesas group, I knew the few islands in the group were a long way apart and the sea thundered unchecked against perpendicular cliffs where we should have to keep our eyes open while steering for the mouths of the few valleys, which always ended in strips of beach.

If, on the contrary, she headed down toward the coral reefs of the Tuamotu group, there the numerous islands lay close together and covered a wide space of sea. But this group of islands is also known as the Low or Dangerous Archipelago, because the whole formation has been built up entirely by coral polyps and consists of treacherous submerged reefs and palm-clad atolls which rise only six or ten feet

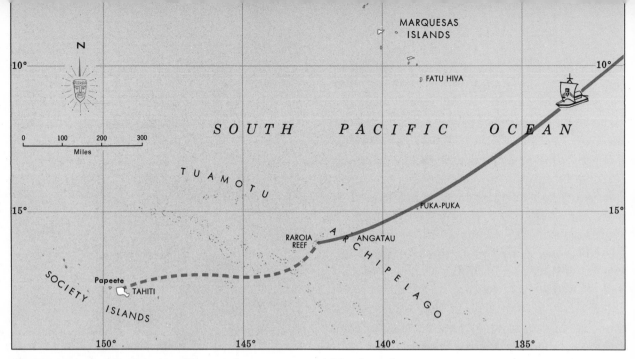

The Tuamoto Archipelago is made up of numerous coral islands and atolls surrounded by treacherous submerged reefs.

above the surface of the sea. Dangerous ring-shaped reefs fling themselves protectingly round every single atoll and are a menace to shipping throughout the area. But, even if coral polyps built the Tuamotu atolls while the Marquesas Islands are remains of extinct volcanoes, both groups are inhabited by the same Polynesian race, and the royal families in both regard Tiki as their ancestor.

MESSENGER FROM POLYNESIA

As early as July 3, when we were still 1,000 sea miles from Polynesia, Nature herself was able to tell us, as she was able to tell the primitive raftsmen from Peru in their time, that there really was land ahead somewhere out in the sea. Until we were a good thousand sea miles out from the coast of Peru we had noted small flocks of frigate birds. They disappeared at about 100° west, and after that we saw only small petrels which have their home on the sea. But on July 3 the frigate birds reappeared, at 125° west, and from now onward small flocks of frigate birds were often to be seen, either high up in the sky or shooting down over the wave crests, where they snapped up flying fish which had taken to the air to escape from dolphins. As these birds did not come from America astern of us, they must have their homes in some country ahead.

On July 16 Nature betrayed herself still more obviously. On that day we hauled up a nine-foot shark, which threw up from its stomach a large undigested starfish which it had recently brought from some coast out here in the ocean.

And the very next day we had the first definite visitor straight from the islands of Polynesia.

It was a great moment on board when two large boobies were spotted above the horizon to westward and soon afterward came sailing in over our mast, flying low. With a wing-spread of five feet they circled round us many times, then folded their wings and settled on the sea alongside us. Dolphins rushed to the spot at once and wriggled inquisitively round the great swimming birds, but neither party touched the other. These were the first living messengers that came to bid us welcome to Polynesia. They did not go back in the evening but rested on the sea, and after midnight we still heard them flying in circles round the mast, uttering hoarse cries.

The flying fish which came on board were now of another and much larger species; I recognized them from fishing trips I had taken with the natives along the coast of Fatu Hiva.

For three days and nights we made straight toward Fatu Hiva, but then a strong northeast wind came on and sent us down in the direction of the Tuamotu atolls. We were now blown out of the real South Equatorial Current, and the ocean currents were no longer behaving dependably. One day they were there; another day they were gone. The currents could run like invisible rivers branching out all over the sea. If the current was swift, there was usually more swell and the temperature of the water usually fell one degree. It showed its direction and strength every day by the difference between Erik's calculated and his measured position.

On the threshold of Polynesia the wind said "Pass," having handed us over to a weak branch of the current which, to our alarm, had its course in the direction of the Antarctic. The wind did not become absolutely still—we never experienced that throughout the voyage—and when it was feeble we hoisted every rag we had to collect what little there was. There was not one day on which we moved backward toward America, and our smallest distance in twenty-four hours was 9 sea miles, while our average run for the voyage as a whole was 42½ sea miles in twenty-four hours.

The trade wind, after all, had not the heart to fail us right in the last lap. It reported for duty again and pushed and shoved at the ramshackle craft which was preparing her entry into a new and strange part of the world.

With each day that passed, larger flocks of sea birds came and circled over us aimlessly in all directions. One evening, when the sun was about to sink into the sea, we noticed that the birds had received a violent impetus. They were flying away in a westerly direction without paying any attention to us or the flying fish beneath them. From the masthead we could see that, as they came over, they all flew straight on on exactly the same course. Perhaps they saw something from up above which we did not see. Perhaps they were flying by instinct. In any case they were flying with a plan, straight home to the nearest island, their breeding place.

We twisted the steering oar and set our course exactly in the direction in which the birds had disappeared. Even after it was dark, we heard the cries of stragglers flying over us against the starry sky on exactly the same course as that which we were now following. It was a wonderful night; the moon was nearly

Sea birds of the Pacific.
Top: Red-footed booby
Left: Frigate bird
Right: Petrel

full for the third time in the course of the *Kon-Tiki's* voyage.

Next day there were still more birds over us, but we did not need to wait for them to show us our way again in the evening. This time we had detected a curious stationary cloud above the horizon. The other clouds were small feathery wisps of wool which came up in the south and passed across the vault of the sky with the trade wind till they disappeared over the horizon in the west. So I had once come to know the drifting trade-wind clouds on Fatu Hiva, and so we had seen them over us night and day on board the *Kon-Tiki*. But the lonely cloud on the horizon to the southwest did not move; it just rose like a motionless column of smoke while the trade-wind clouds drifted by. The Polynesians knew land lay under such clouds. For, when the tropical sun bakes the hot sand, a stream of warm air is created which rises up and causes its vapor content to condense up in the colder strata of air.

We steered on the cloud till it disappeared after sunset. The wind was steady, and with the steering oar lashed tight the *Kon-Tiki* kept to her course unaided. The steering watch's job was now to sit on the plank at the masthead, shiny with wear, and keep a lookout for anything that indicated land.

There was a deafening screaming of birds over us all that night. And the moon was nearly full.

At dawn on July 30 we had our first glimpse of Polynesia. The little island on the horizon was Puka Puka, one of the coral islands of the Tuamoto Archipelago.

7. South Sea Islands

ON THE NIGHT before July 30 there was a new and strange atmosphere about the *Kon-Tiki*. Perhaps it was the deafening clamor from all the sea birds over us which showed that something fresh was brewing. The screaming of birds with many voices sounded hectic and earthly after the dead creaking of lifeless ropes, which was all we had heard above the noise of the sea in the three months we had behind us. And the moon seemed larger and rounder than ever as it sailed over the lookout at the masthead.

At six o'clock Bengt came down from the masthead, woke Herman, and turned in. When Herman clambered up the creaking, swaying mast, the day had begun to break. Ten minutes later he was down the rope ladder again and was shaking me by the leg.

"Come out and have a look at your island!"

His face was radiant and I jumped up, followed by Bengt who had not quite gone to sleep yet. Hard on one another's heels, we huddled together as high as we could climb, at the point where the masts crossed. There were many birds around us. Over the whole horizon away to the east a ruddy glow had begun to spread, and far down to the southeast it gradually formed a blood-red background for a faint shadow, like a blue pencil line, drawn for a short way along the edge of the sea.

LAND!

Land! An island! We devoured it greedily with our eyes and woke the others, who tumbled out drowsily and stared in all directions as if they thought our bow was about to run on to a beach. Screaming sea birds formed a bridge across the sky in the direction of the distant island, which stood out sharper against the horizon as the red background widened and turned gold with the approach of the sun and the full daylight.

119

Our first thought was that the island did not lie where it should. As the island could not have drifted, the raft must have been caught up in a northward current in the course of the night. We had only to cast one glance over the sea to perceive at once, from the direction of the waves, that we had lost our chance in the darkness. Where we now lay, the wind no longer allowed us to press the raft on a course toward the island. The region round the Tuamotu Archipelago was full of strong, local ocean currents which twisted in all directions as they ran up against land; many of them varied in direction as they met powerful tidal currents flowing in and out over reefs and lagoons.

We laid the steering oar over, but we knew quite well that it was useless. At half-past six the sun rose out of the sea and climbed straight up as it does in the tropics. The island lay some few sea miles away and had the appearance of a quite low strip of forest creeping along the horizon. The trees were crowded close together behind a narrow light-colored beach, which lay so low that it was hidden behind the seas at regular intervals. According to Erik's positions this island was Puka Puka, the first outpost of the Tuamotu group. *Sailing Directions for Pacific Islands—1940,* our two different charts, and Erik's observations gave, in all, four quite different positions for this island, but as there were no other islands in all that neighborhood there could be no doubt that the island we saw was Puka Puka.

No extravagant outbursts were to be heard on board. After the sail had been trimmed and the oar laid over, we all formed a silent group at the masthead or stood on deck staring toward the land which had suddenly cropped up out in the middle of the endless sea. At last we had a visible proof that we had really been moving in all these months; we had not just been lying tumbling about in the center of the same eternal circular horizon. To us it seemed as if the island were mobile and had suddenly entered the circle of blue and empty sea in the center of which we had our permanent abode; as if the island were drifting slowly across our own domain, heading for the eastern horizon. We were all filled with a warm, quiet satisfaction at having actually reached Polynesia, mingled with a faint momentary disappointment at having to submit helplessly to seeing the island lie there like a mirage while we continued our eternal drift across the sea westward.

Just after sunrise a thick black column of smoke rose above the treetops to the left of the middle of the island. We followed it with our eyes and thought to ourselves that the natives were rising and getting their breakfast. We had no idea then that native lookout posts had seen us and were sending up smoke signals to invite us to land. About seven o'clock we scented a faint breath of burned *borao* wood which tickled our salted nostrils. It awoke in me at once slumbering memories of the fire on the beach on Fatu Hiva. Half an hour later we caught the smell of newly cut wood and of forest. The island had now begun to shrink and lay astern of us so that we received flickering wafts of breeze from it. For a quarter of an hour Herman and I clung to the masthead and let the warm smell of leaves and greenery filter in through our nostrils. This was Polynesia—a beautiful, rich smell of dry land after ninety-three salty days down among the waves. Bengt already lay snoring in his sleeping bag again. Erik and Torstein lay on their backs in the cabin thinking, and Knut ran in and out and sniffed the smell of leaves and wrote in his diary.

PUKA PUKA DISAPPEARS

At half-past eight Puka Puka sank into the sea astern of us, but right on till eleven o'clock we could see, on climbing to the masthead, that there was a faint blue streak above the horizon in the east. Then that too was gone, and a high cloud, rising motionless skyward, was all that showed where Puka Puka lay. The birds disappeared. They kept by preference to windward of the islands so that they had the wind with them when they returned home in the evening with full bellies. The dolphins also had become noticeably scarcer, and there were again only a few pilot fish under the raft.

Land ahead! As we neared the French island of Angatau, we hoisted all our flags and prepared for the end of our voyage.

That night Bengt said he longed for a table and chair, for it was so tiring to lie and turn from back to stomach while reading. Otherwise he was glad we had missed our landing, for he still had three books to read. Torstein suddenly had a desire for an apple, and I myself woke up in the night because I definitely smelled a delicious odor of steak and onions. But it turned out to be only a dirty shirt.

The very next morning we detected two new clouds rising up like the steam from two locomotives below the horizon. The map was able to tell us that the names of the coral islands they came from were Fangahina and Angatau. The cloud over Angatau lay the most favorably for us as the wind was blowing, so we set our course for that, lashed the oar fast, and enjoyed the wonderful peace and freedom of the Pacific. So lovely was life on this fine day on the bamboo deck of the *Kon-Tiki* that we drank in all the impressions in the certainty that the journey would soon be over now, whatever might await us.

For three days and nights we steered on the cloud over Angatau; the weather was brilliant, the oar alone held us on our course, and the current played us no tricks. On the fourth morning Torstein relieved Herman after the 4–6 watch and was told that Herman thought he had seen the outlines of a low island in the moonlight. When the sun rose just afterward, Torstein stuck his head in at the cabin door and shouted:

"Land ahead!"

LAND AGAIN!

We all plunged out on deck, and what we saw made us hoist all our flags. First the Norwegian aft, then the French at the masthead because we were heading for a French colony. Soon the raft's entire collection of flags was fluttering in the fresh trade wind—the American, British, Peruvian, and Swedish flags besides the flag of the Explorers Club—so there was no doubt on board that now the *Kon-Tiki* was dressed. The island was ideally placed

A dangerous reef with seething breakers barred our approach to the island.

this time, right in our own course and a little farther away from us than Puka Puka had been when it cropped up at sunrise four days before. As the sun rose straight up over the sky astern of us, we could see a clear green glimmer high up toward the misty sky over the island. It was the reflection of the still, green lagoon on the inside of the surrounding reef.

· About ten o'clock we took charge of the steering oar ourselves; we must now decide toward which part of the island we should steer. We could already distinguish individual treetops from the others and could see rows of tree trunks shining in the sun, which stood out against the background of dense foliage.

We knew that somewhere between us and the island there was a dangerous submerged shoal, lying in ambush for anything that approached the innocent island. This reef lay right under the deep, free roll of the swell from the east, and, as the huge masses of water lost their balance above the shoal, they wavered skyward and plunged down, thundering and foaming, over the sharp coral reef. Many vessels have been caught in the terrible suction against the submerged reefs in the Tuamotu group and have been smashed to pieces.

From the sea we saw nothing of this trap. We sailed in, following the direction of the waves, and saw only the curved shining back of sea after sea disappearing toward the island. Both the reef and the whole frothing witches' dance over it were hidden behind rising rows of broad wave backs ahead of us. But along both ends of the island where we saw the beach in profile, both north and south, we saw

that a few hundred yards from land the sea was one white boiling mass flinging itself high into the air.

We laid our course so as to graze the outside of the witches' kitchen off the southern point of the island, hoping, when we got there, to be able to steer along the atoll till we came round the point on the lee side or till we touched, before we drifted past, a place where it was so shallow that we could stop our drift with a makeshift anchor and wait till the wind changed and placed us under the lee of the island.

About noon we could see through the glass that the vegetation on shore consisted of young green coconut palms, which stood with their tops close together over a waving hedge of luxuriant undergrowth in the foreground. On the beach in front of them a number of large coral blocks lay strewn about on the bright sand. Otherwise there was no sign of life, apart from white birds sailing over the palm tufts.

At two o'clock we had come so close that we began to sail along the island, just outside the baffling reef. As we gradually approached, we heard the roar of the breakers like a steady waterfall against the reef, and soon they sounded like an endless express train running parallel with us a few hundred yards from our starboard side.

Two men at the same time stood turning the steering oar; they were behind the bamboo cabin and so had no view ahead whatever. Erik, as navigator, stood on the top of the kitchen box and gave directions to the two men at the heavy oar. Our plan was to keep as close in to the dangerous reef as was safe. We kept a continuous lookout from the masthead for a gap or opening in the reef where we could try to slip the raft through. The current was now driving us along the whole length of the reef and played us no tricks. The loose centerboards allowed us to steer at an angle of about 20° to the wind on both sides, and the wind was blowing along the reef.

While Erik directed our zigzag course and took his loops as near the reef as was advisable in view of the suction, Herman and I went out in the rubber dinghy at the end of a rope.

When the raft was on the inward tack, we swung after her on the rope and came so close to the thundering reef that we caught a glimpse of the glass-green wall of water that was rolling away from us and saw how, when the seas sucked themselves back, the naked reef exposed itself, resembling a torn-up barricade of rusty iron ore. As far as we could see along the coast there was no gap or passage. So Erik trimmed the sail by tightening the port and loosening the starboard sheets, and the helmsman followed with the steering oar, so that the *Kon-Tiki* turned her nose out again and tumbled away from the danger zone till her next drive inward.

THE COAST OF ANGATAU

Each time the *Kon-Tiki* stood in toward the reef and swung out again, we two who were in tow in the dinghy sat with our hearts in our mouths, for each time we came so close in that we felt the beat of the seas becoming nervous as it rose higher and fiercer. And each time we were convinced that this time Erik had gone too far, that this time there was no hope of getting the *Kon-Tiki* out again clear of the breakers which drew us in toward the devilish red reef. But each time Erik got clear

with a smart maneuver, and the *Kon-Tiki* ran safely out into the open sea again, well out of the clutch of the suction. All the time we were gliding along the island, so close that we saw every detail on shore.

About three o'clock the forest of palms ashore opened, and through a wide gap we saw right into a blue glassy lagoon. But the surrounding reef lay as compact as ever, gnashing its blood-red teeth ominously in the foam. There was no passage, and the palm forest closed again as we plodded on along the island with the wind at our backs. Later the palm forest became thinner and thinner and gave us a view into the interior of the coral island. This consisted of the fairest, brightest saltwater lagoon, surrounded by swaying coconut palms and shining bathing beaches. The green palm island itself formed a broad, soft ring of sand round the hospitable lagoon, and a second ring ran round the whole island—the rust-red reef which prevented our landing.

All day we zigzagged along Angatau and had its beauty at close quarters, just outside the cabin door. The sun beat down on all the palms, and all was Paradise and joy on the island within. As our maneuvers gradually became a matter of routine, Erik got out his

Although we could not land, Erik celebrated our arrival in Polynesia with a guitar serenade.

The bearded crew of the *Kon-Tiki*. Left to right: Erik, Torstein, Bengt, the author, Knut. Herman was the photographer.

guitar and stood on deck in a huge Peruvian sun hat playing and singing sentimental South Sea songs, while Bengt served an excellent dinner on the edge of the raft. We opened an old coconut from Peru and drank to the young fresh nuts which hung on the trees inside. The whole atmosphere—the peace over the bright, green palm forest which stood deep-rooted and beckoned toward us, the peace over the white birds that sailed round the palm tops, the peace over the glassy lagoon and the soft sand beach, and the viciousness of the red reef, the cannonading and roll of drums in the air—all made an overwhelming impression on the six of us who had come in from the sea. There was no doubt that now we had reached the other side; we should never see a more genuine South Sea island. Landing or no landing, we had nonetheless reached Polynesia; the expanse of sea lay behind us for all time.

THE 97TH DAY

It happened that this festal day off Angatau was the ninety-seventh day on board. Strangely enough, it was ninety-seven days that we had estimated in New York as the absolute minimum time in which, in theoretically ideal conditions, we could reach the nearest islands of Polynesia.

At half-past five we stood in toward the reef again; we had sailed along the whole south coast and were getting near the west end of the island, and must have a last look round in the hope of finding a passage before we passed. The sun now stood so low that it blinded us when we looked ahead, but we saw a little rainbow in the air where the sea broke against the reef a few hundred yards beyond the last point of the island. This now lay as a silhouette ahead of us. On the beach inside we detected a cluster of motionless black spots. Suddenly one of them moved slowly down toward the water, while several of the others made off at full speed up to the edge of the woods. They were people! We steered along the reef as close in as we dared; the wind had died down so that we felt we were within an inch of getting under the lee of the island. Now we saw a canoe being launched, and two individuals jumped on board and paddled off on the other side of the reef. Farther down they turned the boat's head out, and we saw the canoe lifted high in the air by the seas as it shot through a passage in the reef and came straight out toward us.

The opening in the reef, then, was down there; there was our only hope. Now, too, we could see the whole village lying in among the palm trunks. But the shadows were already growing long.

THE FIRST NATIVES

The two men in the canoe waved. We waved back eagerly, and they increased their speed. It was a Polynesian outrigger canoe; two brown figures in singlets sat paddling, facing ahead. Now there would be fresh language difficulties. I alone of those on board remembered a few words of Marquesan from my stay on Fatu Hiva, but Polynesian is a difficult language to keep up, for lack of practice in our northern countries.

We felt some relief, therefore, when the canoe bumped against the raft's side and the two men leaped on board, for one of them grinned all over his face and held out a brown hand, exclaiming in English:

"Good night!"

"Good night," I replied in astonishment. "Do you speak English?"

The man grinned again and nodded.

"Good night," he said. "Good night."

This was his entire vocabulary in foreign languages, and thereby he scored heavily over his more modest friend, who just stood in the background and grinned, much impressed, at his experienced comrade.

"Angatau?" I asked, pointing toward the island.

"H'angatau," the man nodded affirmatively.

Erik nodded proudly. He had been right; we were where the sun had told him that we were.

"*Maimai hee iuta,*" I tried.

According to my knowledge acquired on Fatu Hiva this should mean approximately, "Want to go to land."

They both pointed toward the invisible passage in the reef, and we laid the oar over and decided to take our chance.

At that moment fresher gusts of wind came from the interior of the island. A small rain cloud lay over the lagoon. The wind threatened to force us away from the reef, and we saw that the *Kon-Tiki* was not answering the steering oar at a wide enough angle to be able to reach the mouth of the opening in the reef. We tried to find bottom, but the anchor rope was not long enough. Now we had to have resort to the paddles, and pretty quickly, too, before the wind got a fair hold of us. We hauled down the sail at top speed and each of us got out his big paddle.

I wanted to give an extra paddle to each of the two natives, who stood enjoying the cigarettes they had been given on board. They only shook their heads vigorously, pointed out the course, and looked confused. I made signs that we must all paddle and repeated the words, "Want to go to land!" Then the most advanced of the two bent down, made a cranking motion in the air with his right hand, and said: "*Brrrrrrrrr-!*"

There was no doubt whatever that he wanted us to start the engine. They thought they were standing on the deck of a curiously deep-loaded boat. We took them aft and made them feel under the logs to show them that we had no propeller or screw. They were

Natives in outrigger canoes came out from Angatau to welcome us and invite us ashore.

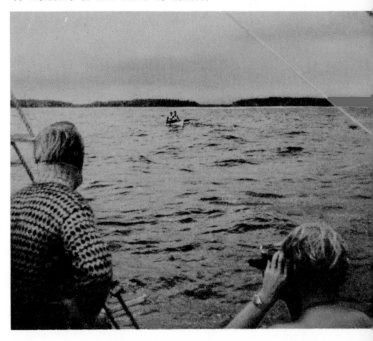

dumbfounded and, putting out their cigarettes, flung themselves down on the side of the raft where we sat—four men on each outside log, dipping our paddles into the water. At the same time the sun sank straight into the sea behind the point, and the gusts of wind from the interior of the island freshened. It did not look as if we were moving an inch. The natives looked frightened, jumped back into the canoe, and disappeared. It grew dark, and we were alone once more, paddling desperately so as not to drift out to sea again.

As darkness fell over the island, four canoes came dancing out from behind the reef, and soon there was a crowd of Polynesians on board, all wanting to shake hands and get cigarettes. With these fellows on board, who had local knowledge, there was no danger. They would not let us go out to sea again and out of sight, so we should be ashore that evening!

We quickly had ropes made fast from the sterns of all the canoes to the bow of the *Kon-Tiki*, and the four sturdy outrigger canoes spread out in fan formation, like a dog team, ahead of the wooden raft. Knut jumped into the dinghy and found a place as draft dog in among the canoes, and we others, with paddles, posted ourselves on the two outside logs of the *Kon-Tiki*. And so began, for the first time, a struggle against the east wind which had been at our back for so long.

It was now pitch dark until the moon rose, and there was a fresh wind. On land the inhabitants of the village had collected brushwood and lighted a big fire to show us the direction of the passage through the reef. The thundering from the reef surrounded us in the darkness like a ceaselessly roaring waterfall, and at first the noise grew louder and louder.

We could not see the team that was pulling us in the canoes ahead, but we heard them singing exhilarating war songs in Polynesian at the top of their lungs. We could hear that Knut was with them, for every time the Polynesian music died away we heard Knut's solitary voice singing Norwegian folk songs in the midst of the Polynesian's chorus. To complete the chaos we on board the raft chimed in with "Tom Brown's baby had a pimple on his nose," and both white and brown men heaved at their paddles with laughter and song.

We were overflowing with high spirits. Ninety-seven days. Arrived in Polynesia. There would be a feast in the village that evening. The natives cheered and bellowed and shouted. There was a landing on Angatau only once a year, when the copra schooner came from Tahiti to fetch coconut kernels. So there would indeed be a feast round the fire on land that evening.

But the angry wind blew stubbornly. We toiled till every limb ached. We held our

A Polynesian outrigger canoe.

ground, but the fire did not come any nearer and the thunder from the reef was just the same as before. Gradually the singing died away. All grew still. It was all and more than the men could do to row. The fire did not move; it only danced up and down as we fell and rose with the seas. Three hours passed, and it was now nine o'clock. Gradually we began to lose ground. We were tired.

We made the natives understand that we needed more help from land. They explained to us that there were plenty of people ashore, but they had only these four seagoing canoes in the whole island.

Then Knut appeared out of the darkness with the dinghy. He had an idea; he could row in in the rubber dinghy and fetch more natives. Five or six men could sit crowded together in the dinghy at a pinch.

This was too risky. Knut had no local knowledge; he would never be able to feel his way forward to the opening in the coral reef in that pitch-black darkness. He then proposed to take with him the leader of the natives, who could show him the way. I did not think this plan a safe one, either, for the native had no experience in maveuvering a clumsy rubber dinghy through the narrow and dangerous passage. But I asked Knut to fetch the leader, who was sitting paddling in the darkness ahead of us, so that we might hear what he thought of the situation.

Knut disappeared into the darkness to find the leader. When some time had passed and Knut had not returned with the leader, we shouted for them but received no answer except from a cackling chorus of Polynesians ahead. Knut had vanished into the darkness. At that moment we understood what had happened. In all the bustle, noise, and turmoil Knut had misunderstood his instructions and rowed shoreward with the leader. All our shouting was useless, for where Knut now was all other sounds were drowned by the thunder all along the barrier.

We quickly got hold of a Morse lamp, and a man climbed up to the masthead and signaled, "Come back. Come back."

But no one came back.

With two men away and one continuously signaling at the masthead our drift astern increased, and the rest of us had begun to grow really tired. We threw marks overboard and saw that we were moving slowly but surely the wrong way. The fire grew smaller and the noise from the breakers less. And the farther we emerged from under the lee of the palm forest, the firmer hold of us the eternal east wind took. We felt it again now; it was almost as it had been out at sea. We gradually realized that all hope had gone—we were drifting out to sea. But we must not slacken our paddling. We must put the brake on the drift astern with all our might till Knut was safe on board again.

Five minutes went. Ten minutes. Half an hour. The fire grew smaller; now and then it disappeared altogether when we ourselves slid down into the trough of the sea. The breakers became a distant murmur. Now the moon rose; we could just see the glimmer of its disk behind the palm tops on land, but the sky seemed misty and half clouded over. We heard the natives beginning to murmur and exchange words. Suddenly we noticed that one of the canoes had cast off its rope into the sea and disappeared. The men in the other three canoes were tired and frightened and were no longer pulling their full weight. The *Kon-Tiki* went on drifting out over the open sea.

Soon the three remaining ropes slackened and the three canoes bumped against the side of the raft. One of the natives came on board and said quietly with a jerk of his head:

"*Iuta* (To land)."

He looked anxiously at the fire, which now disappeared for long periods at a time and only flashed out now and again like a spark. We were drifting fast. The breakers were silent; only the sea roared as it used to, and all the ropes on board the *Kon-Tiki* creaked and groaned.

We plied the natives with cigarettes, and I hurriedly scrawled a note which they were to take with them and give to Knut if they found him. It ran:

Take two natives with you in a canoe with

the dinghy in tow. Do NOT come back in the dinghy alone.

We counted on the helpful islanders being willing to take Knut with them in a canoe, assuming they thought it advisable to put to sea at all; if they did not think it advisable, it would be madness for Knut to venture out on to the ocean in the dinghy in the hope of overtaking the runaway raft.

The natives took the scrap of paper, jumped into the canoes, and disappeared into the night. The last we heard was the shrill voice of our first friend out in the darkness calling politely:

"Good night!"

There was a murmur of appreciation from the others, and then all was as silent, as free from sounds from without as when we were 2,000 sea miles from the nearest land.

It was useless for us four to do anything more with the paddles out here in the open sea, under the full pressure of the wind, but we continued the light signals from the masthead. We dared not send "Come back" any longer; we now sent out only regular flashes. It was pitch dark. The moon appeared only through occasional rifts in the bank of clouds.

At ten o'clock we gave up the last faint hope of seeing Knut again. We sat down in silence on the edge of the raft and munched a few biscuits, while we took turns flashing signals from the masthead, which seemed just a naked projection without the broad *Kon-Tiki* sail.

We decided to keep the lamp-signaling going all night, so long as we did not know where Knut was. We refused to believe that he had been caught by the breakers. Knut always landed on his feet, whether it was heavy water or breakers; he was alive, all right. Only it was unbearable to have him stuck down among Polynesians on an out-of-the-way island in the Pacific. What a situation! After all that long voyage, all we could do was to nip in and land a man on a remote South Sea island and sail off again. Indeed, no sooner had the first Polynesians come smiling on board than they had to clear out headlong to escape being themselves caught up in the *Kon-*

Tiki's wild rush westward. It all seemed so silly to the five of us left on board. And the ropes were creaking horribly that night. Not one of us showed a sign of wanting to sleep.

It was half-past ten. Bengt was coming down to be relieved at the swaying masthead. Then we all started. We had heard voices clearly, out on the sea in the darkness. There it was again. It was Polynesians talking. We shouted into the black night with all the strength of our lungs. They shouted back, and —there was Knut's voice among the rest! We were mad with excitement. Our tiredness had gone; the whole thundercloud had lifted. What did it matter if we drifted away from Angatau? There were other islands in the sea. Now the nine balsa logs, so fond of travel, could drift where they liked, so long as all six of us were assembled on board again.

Three outrigger canoes emerged from the darkness, riding over the swell, and Knut was the first man to jump across to the dear old *Kon-Tiki*, followed by six brown men. There was little time for explanations; the natives must have presents and be off on their adventurous journey back to the island. Without seeing light or land, and with hardly any stars, they had to find their course by paddling against wind and sea till they saw the light from the fire. We rewarded them amply with provisions, cigarettes, and other gifts, and each of them shook us heartily by the hand in a last farewell.

They were clearly anxious on our account; they pointed westward, indicating that we were heading toward dangerous reefs. The leader had tears in his eyes and kissed me tenderly on the chin, which made me thank Providence for my beard. Then they crept into the canoes, and we six comrades were left on the raft, together and alone.

We left the raft to her own devices and listened to Knut's story.

Knut had in good faith made for land in the dinghy with the native leader on board. The native himself was sitting at the little oars and rowing toward the opening in the reef, when Knut to his surprise saw the light signals from the *Kon-Tiki* asking him to come back.

Welcome back! Knut rejoining the raft after almost being stranded on Angatau.

He made signs to the rower to turn, but the native refused to obey. Then Knut took hold of the oars himself, but the native tore his hands away, and with the reef thundering round them it was no use starting a fight. They had bounded right in through the opening in the reef and gone on inside it, until they were lifted right up on to a solid coral block on the island itself. A crowd of natives caught hold of the dinghy and dragged it high up on the shore, and Knut stood alone under the palm trees surrounded by a huge crowd of natives chattering away in an unknown lingo. Brown, barelegged men, women, and children of all ages flocked round him and felt the material of his shirt and trousers. They themselves wore ragged old European clothes, but there were no white men on the island.

Knut got hold of some of the smartest fellows and made signs to them that they should go out in the dinghy with him. Then a big fat man came waddling up who Knut presumed must be the chief, for he had an old uniform cap on his head and talked in a loud, authoritative voice. All made way for him. Knut explained both in Norwegian and in English that he needed men and must get back to the raft before we others drifted away. The chief beamed and understood nothing, and Knut, despite his most vehement protests, was pushed over to the village by the whole shout-

ing crowd. There he was received by dogs and pigs and pretty South Sea girls who came along carrying fresh fruit. It was clear that the natives were prepared to make Knut's stay as agreeable as possible, but Knut was not to be enticed; he thought sadly of the raft which was vanishing westward. The natives' intention was obvious. They badly wanted our company, and they knew that there were a lot of good things on board white men's ships. If they could keep Knut ashore, the rest of us and the queer boat would certainly come in also. No vessel would leave a white man behind on such an out-of-the-way island as Angatau.

After more curious experiences Knut got away and hurried down to the dinghy, surrounded by admirers of both sexes. His international speech and gesticulations could no longer be misunderstood; they realized that he must and would return to the odd craft out in the night, which was in such a hurry that she had to go on at once.

Then the natives tried a trick; they indicated by signs that the rest of us were coming ashore on the other side of the point. Knut was puzzled for a few minutes, but then loud voices were heard down on the beach, where women and children were tending the flickering fire. The three canoes had come back, and the men brought Knut the note. He was in a desperate situation. Here were instructions not to row out on the sea alone, and all the natives absolutely refused to go with him.

There followed a high-pitched, noisy argument among all the natives. Those who had been out and seen the raft understood perfectly well that it was of little use to keep Knut back in the hope of getting the rest of us ashore. The end of it was that Knut's promises and threats in international accents induced the crews of three canoes to accompany him out to sea in pursuit of the *Kon-Tiki*. They put out to sea in the tropical night with the dinghy dancing along in tow, while the natives stood motionless by the dying fire and watched their new blond friend disappear as quickly as he had come.

Knut and his companions could see the faint light signals from the raft far out to sea when the swell lifted the canoes. The long, slim Polynesian canoes, stiffened by an outrigger each, cut through the water like knives, but it seemed an eternity to Knut before he felt the thick round logs of the *Kon-Tiki* under his feet again.

"Have a good time ashore?" Torstein asked enviously.

OUT TO SEA AGAIN

We left the sail down and the oar inboard, and all six of us crept into the bamboo cabin and slept like boulders on the beach at Angatau.

For three days we drifted across the sea without a sight of land.

We were drifting straight toward the ominous Takume and Raroia reefs, which together blocked up forty to fifty miles of the sea ahead of us. We made desperate efforts to steer clear, to the north of these dangerous reefs, and things seemed to be going well till one night the watch came hurrying in and called us all out.

The wind had changed. We were heading straight for the Takume reef. It had begun to rain, and there was no visibility at all. The reef could not be far off.

In the middle of night we held a council of war. It was a question of saving our lives

now. To get past on the north side was now hopeless; we must try to get through on the south side instead. We trimmed the sail, laid the oar over, and began a dangerous piece of sailing with the uncertain north wind behind us. If the east wind came back before we had passed the whole façade of the fifty-mile-long reefs, we should be hurled in among the breakers, at their mercy.

We agreed on all that should be done if shipwreck was imminent. We would stay on board the *Kon-Tiki* at all costs. We would not climb up the mast, from which we should be shaken down like rotten fruit, but would cling tight to the stays of the mast when the seas poured over us. We laid the rubber raft loose on the deck and made fast to it a small watertight radio transmitter, a small quantity of provisions, waterbottles, and medical stores. This would be washed ashore independently of us if we ourselves should get over the reef safe but emptyhanded. In the stern of the *Kon-Tiki* we made fast a long rope with a float which also would be washed ashore, so that we could try to pull in the raft if she were stranded out on the reef. And so we crept into bed and left the watch to the helmsman out in the rain.

As long as the north wind held, we glided slowly but surely down along the facade of the coral reefs which lay in ambush below the horizon. But then one afternoon the wind died away, and when it returned it had gone round into the east. According to Erik's position, we were already so far down that we now had some hope of steering clear of the southernmost point of the Raroia reef. We would try to get round it and into shelter before going on to other reefs beyond it.

When night came, we had been a hundred days at sea.

DANGEROUS WATERS

Late in the night I woke, feeling restless and uneasy. There was something unusual in the movement of the waves. The *Kon-Tiki's* motion was a little different from what it usually was in such conditions. We had become sensitive to changes in the rhythm of the logs.

I thought at once of suction from a coast, which was drawing near, and was continually out on deck and up the mast. Nothing but sea was visible. But I could get no quiet sleep. Time passed.

At dawn, just before six, Torstein came hurrying down from the masthead. He could see a whole line of small palm-clad islands far ahead. Before doing anything else we laid the oar over to southward as far as we could. What Torstein had seen must be the small coral islands which lay strewn like pearls on a string behind the Raroia reef. A northward current must have caught us.

At half-past seven palm-clad islets had appeared in a row all along the horizon to westward. The southernmost lay roughly ahead of our bow, and thence there were islands and clumps of palms all along the horizon on our starboard side till they disappeared as dots away to northward. The nearest were four or five sea miles away.

A survey from the masthead showed that, even if our bow pointed toward the bottom island in the chain, our drift sideways was so great that we were not advancing in the direction in which our bow pointed. We were drifting diagonally right in toward the reef. With fixed centerboards we should still have had some hope of steering clear. But sharks were following close astern, so that it was impossible to dive under the raft and tighten up the loose centerboards with fresh guy ropes.

We saw that we had now only a few hours more on board the *Kon-Tiki*. They must be used in preparation for our inevitable wreck on the coral reef. Every man learned what he had to do when the moment came; each one of us knew where his own responsibility lay, so that we should not fly round treading on one another's toes when the time came and seconds counted. The *Kon-Tiki* pitched up and down, up and down, as the wind forced us in. There was no doubt that here was the turmoil of waves created by the reef—some waves advancing while others were hurled back after beating vainly against the surrounding wall.

We were still under full sail in the hope of even now being able to steer clear. As we

From the masthead we could see that we were drifting directly toward a dangerous coral reef.

gradually drifted nearer, half sideways, we saw from the mast how the whole string of palm-clad isles was connected with a coral reef, part above and part under water.

I knew what awaited us; I had visited the Tuamotu group before and had seen the size of the giant Pacific surf from the land side.

On board the *Kon-Tiki* all preparations for the end of the voyage were being made. Everything of value was carried into the cabin and lashed fast. Documents and papers were packed into watertight bags, along with films and other things which would not stand a dip in the sea. The whole bamboo cabin was covered with canvas, and especially strong ropes were lashed across it. When we saw that all hope was gone, we opened up the bamboo deck and cut off with machete knives all the ropes which held the centerboards down. It was a hard job to get the centerboards drawn

131

up, because they were all thickly covered with stout barnacles. With the centerboards up the draught of our vessel was no deeper than to the bottom of the timber logs, and we would therefore be more easily washed in over the reef. With no centerboards and with the sail down, the raft lay completely sideways on and was entirely at the mercy of wind and sea.

We tied the longest rope we had to the homemade anchor and made it fast to the step of the port mast, so that the *Kon-Tiki* would go into the surf stern first when the anchor was thrown overboard. The anchor itself consisted of empty water cans filled with used radio batteries and heavy scrap, and solid mangrove-wood sticks projected from it, set crosswise.

Order number one, which came first and last, was: Hold on to the raft! Whatever happened, we must hang on tight on board and let the nine great logs take the pressure from the reef. We ourselves had more than enough to do to withstand the weight of the water. If we jumped overboard, we should become helpless victims of the suction which would fling us in and out over the sharp corals. The rubber raft would capsize in the steep seas or, heavily loaded with us in it, it would be torn to ribbons against the reef. But the wooden logs would sooner or later be cast ashore, and we with them, if we only managed to hold fast.

Next, all hands were told to put on their shoes for the first time in a hundred days and to have their life belts ready. The last precaution, however, was not of much value, for if a man fell overboard he would be battered to death, not drowned. We had time, too, to put our passports and such few dollars as we had left into our pockets. But it was not lack of time that was troubling us.

DRIFTING

Those were anxious hours in which we lay drifting helplessly sideways, step after step, in toward the reef. It was noticeably quiet on board; we all crept silently in and out from cabin to bamboo deck, and carried on with our jobs. Our serious faces showed that no one was in doubt as to what awaited us, and the absence of nervousness showed that we had all gradually acquired an unshakable confidence in the raft. If it had brought us across the sea, it would also manage to bring us ashore alive.

Inside the cabin there was a complete chaos of provision cartons and cargo, lashed fast. Torstein had barely found room for himself in the radio corner, where he had got the short-wave transmitter working. We were now over 4,000 sea miles from our old base at Callao, where the Peruvian Naval War School had maintained regular contact with us, and still farther from Hal and Frank and the other radio amateurs in the United States. But, as chance willed, we had on the previous day got in touch with a capable radio "ham" who had a set on Rarotonga in the Cook Islands, and the operators, quite contrary to all our usual practice, had arranged for an extra contact with him early in the morning. All the time we were drifting closer and closer in to the reef, Torstein was sitting tapping his key and calling Rarotonga.

A few minutes later the anchor rushed overboard and caught hold of the bottom, so that the *Kon-Tiki* swung around and turned her stern inward toward the breakers. It held us for a few valuable minutes, while Torstein sat hammering like mad on the key. He had got Rarotonga now. The breakers thundered in the air and the sea rose and fell furiously. All hands were at work on deck, and now Torstein got his message through. He said we were drifting toward the Raroia reef. He asked Rarotonga to listen in on the same wave length every hour. If we were silent for more than thirty-six hours, Rarotonga must let the Norwegian Embassy in Washington know. Torstein's last words were:

"O.K. Fifty yards left. Here we go. Goodby."

Then he closed down the station, Knut sealed up the papers, and both crawled out on deck as fast as they could to join the rest of us, for it was clear now that the anchor was giving way.

The swell grew heavier and heavier, with deep troughs between the waves, and we felt the raft being swung up and down, up and down, higher and higher.

Again the order was shouted: "Hold on, never mind about the cargo, hold on!"

We were now so near the waterfall inside that we no longer heard the steady continuous roar from all along the reef. We now heard only a separate boom each time the nearest breaker crashed down on the rocks.

All hands stood in readiness, each clinging fast to the rope he thought the most secure. Only Erik crept into the cabin at the last moment; there was one part of the program he had not yet carried out—he had not found his shoes!

No one stood aft, for it was there the shock from the reef would come. Nor were the two firm stays which ran from the masthead down to the stern safe. For if the mast fell they would be left hanging overboard, over the reef. Herman, Bengt, and Torstein had climbed up on some boxes which were lashed fast forward of the cabin wall, and, while Herman clung on to the guy ropes from the ridge of the roof, the other two held on to the ropes from the masthead by which the sail at other times was hauled up. Knut and I chose the stay running from the bow up to the masthead, for, if mast and cabin and everything else went overboard, we thought the rope from the bow would

Hold on! Our only chance was to cling to the raft and hope that it would be washed over the reef by the waves.

nevertheless remain lying inboard, as we were now head on to the seas.

When we realized that the seas had got hold of us, the anchor rope was cut and we were off. A sea rose straight up under us, and we felt the *Kon-Tiki* being lifted up in the air. The great moment had come; we were riding on the wave back at breathless speed, our ramshackle craft creaking and groaning as she quivered under us. The excitement made one's blood boil. I remember that, having no other inspiration, I waved my arm and bellowed "Hurrah!" at the top of my lungs; it afforded a certain relief and could do no harm anyway. The others certainly thought I had gone mad, but they all beamed and grinned enthusiastically. On we ran with the seas rushing in behind us; this was the *Kon-Tiki's* baptism of fire. All must and would go well.

FLOODS OF WATER

But our elation was soon dampened. A new sea rose high up astern of us like a glittering, green glass wall. As we sank down it came rolling after us, and, in the same second in which I saw it high above me, I felt a violent blow and was submerged under floods of water. I felt the suction through my whole body, with such great power that I had to strain every single muscle in my frame and think of one thing only—hold on, hold on! I think that in such a desperate situation the arms will be torn off before the brain consents to let go, evident as the outcome is. Then I felt that the mountain of water was passing on and relaxing its devilish grip of my body. When the whole mountain had rushed on, with an ear-splitting roaring and crashing. I saw Knut again hanging on beside me, doubled up into a ball. Seen from behind, the great sea was almost flat and gray. As it rushed on, it swept over the ridge of the cabin roof which projected from the water, and there hung the three others, pressed against the cabin roof as the water passed over them.

We were still afloat.

In an instant I renewed my hold, with arms and legs bent round the strong rope. Knut let himself down and with a tiger's leap joined the others on the boxes, where the cabin took the strain. I heard reassuring exclamations from them, but at the same time I saw a new green wall rise up and come towering toward us. I shouted a warning and made myself as small and hard as I could where I hung. Then the inferno was over us again. The *Kon-Tiki* disappeared completely under the masses of water. The sea tugged and pulled with all the force it could bring to bear at the poor little bundles of human bodies. The second sea rushed over us, to be followed by a third.

Then I heard a triumphant shout from Knut, who was now hanging on to the rope ladder:

"Look at the raft—she's holding!"

After three seas only the double mast and the cabin had been knocked a bit crooked. Again we had a feeling of triumph over the elements, and the elation of victory gave us new strength.

Then I saw the next sea come towering up, higher than all the rest, and again I bellowed a warning aft to the others as I climbed up the stay, as high as I could get in a hurry, and hung on fast. Then I myself disappeared sideways into the midst of the green wall which towered high over us. The others, who were farther aft and saw me disappear first, estimated the height of the wall of water at twenty-five feet, while the foaming crest passed by fifteen feet above the part of the glassy wall into which I had vanished. Then the great wave reached them, and we had all one single thought—hold on, hold on, hold, hold, hold!

SHIPWRECK

We must have hit the reef that time. I myself felt only the strain on the stay, which seemed to bend and slacken jerkily. But whether the bumps came from above or below I could not tell, hanging there. The whole submersion lasted only seconds, but it demanded more endurance than we usually have in our bodies. There is greater strength in the human mechanism than that of the muscles alone. I determined that, if I was to die, I would die in this position, like a knot on the stay. The sea thundered on, over and past, and

Wrecked on the reef. The raft was shattered, but all of the crew were safe.

as it roared by it revealed a hideous sight. The *Kon-Tiki* was wholly changed, as by the stroke of a magic wand. The vessel we knew from weeks and months at sea was no more; in a few seconds our pleasant world had become a shattered wreck.

I saw only one man on board besides myself. He lay pressed flat across the ridge of the cabin roof, face downward with his arms stretched out on both sides, while the cabin itself was crushed in, like a house of cards, toward the stern and toward the starboard side. The motionless figure was Herman. There was no other sign of life, while the hill of water thundered by, in across the reef. The hardwood mast on the starboard side was broken like a match, and the upper stump, in its fall, had smashed right through the cabin roof, so that the mast and all its gear slanted at a low angle over the reef on the starboard side. Astern, the steering block was twisted round lengthways and the crossbeam broken, while the steering oar was smashed to splinters. The splashboards at the bow were broken like cigar boxes, and the whole deck was torn up and pasted like wet paper against the forward wall of the cabin, along with boxes, cans, canvas, and other cargo. Bamboo sticks and rope ends

The raft was a scene of chaos after the stranding, but it still held together. All hands began the work of salvaging our possessions.

stuck up everywhere, and the general effect was of complete chaos.

I felt cold fear run through my whole body. What was the good of my holding on? If I lost one single man here, in the run in, the whole thing would be ruined, and for the moment there was only one human figure to be seen after the last buffet. In that second Torstein's hunched-up form appeared outside the raft. He was hanging like a monkey in the ropes from the masthead and managed to get onto the logs again, where he crawled up on to the debris forward of the cabin. Herman, too, now turned his head and gave me a forced grin of encouragement, but did not move. I bellowed in the faint hope of locating the others and heard Bengt's calm voice call out that all hands were aboard. They were lying holding on to the ropes behind the tangled barricade which the tough plaiting from the bamboo deck had built up.

All this happened in the course of a few seconds, while the *Kon-Tiki* was being drawn out of the witches' caldron by the backwash, and a fresh sea came rolling over her. For the last time I bellowed "Hang on!" at the top of my lungs amid the uproar, and that was all I

myself did; I hung on and disappeared in the masses of water which rushed over and past in those endless two or three seconds. That was enough for me. I saw the ends of the logs knocking and bumping against a sharp step in the coral reef without going over it. Then we were sucked out again. I also saw the two men who lay stretched out across the ridge of the cabin roof, but none of us smiled any longer. Behind the chaos of bamboo I heard a calm voice call out:

"This won't do."

I myself felt equally discouraged. As the masthead sank farther and farther out over the starboard side, I found myself hanging on to a slack line outside the raft. The next sea came. When it had gone by I was dead tired, and my only thought was to get up onto the logs and lie behind the barricade. When the backwash retreated, I saw for the first time the rugged red reef naked beneath us and perceived Torstein standing, bent double, on gleaming red corals, holding on to a bunch of rope ends from the mast. Knut, standing aft, was about to jump. I shouted that we must all keep on the logs, and Torstein, who had been washed overboard, sprang up again like a cat.

136

CAST ASHORE

Two or three more seas rolled over us with diminishing force, and what happened then I do not remember, except that water foamed in and out and I myself sank lower and lower toward the red reef over which we were being lifted in. Then only crests of foam full of salt spray came whirling in, and I was able to work my way in on to the raft, where we all made for the after end of the logs which was highest up on the reef.

At the same moment Knut crouched down and sprang up on to the reef with the line which lay clear astern. While the backwash was running out, he waded through the whirling water some thirty yards in and stood safely at the end of the line when the next sea foamed in toward him, died down, and ran back from the flat reef like a broad stream.

Then Erik came crawling out of the collapsed cabin, with his shoes on. If we had all done as he did, we should have got off cheaply. As the cabin had not been washed overboard but had been pressed down pretty flat under the canvas, Erik lay quietly stretched out among the cargo and heard the peals of thunder crashing above him while the collapsed bamboo walls curved downward. Bengt had had a slight concussion when the mast fell but had managed to crawl under the wrecked cabin alongside Erik. We should all of us have been lying there if we had realized in advance how firmly the countless lashings and plaited bamboo sheets would hang on to the main logs under the pressure of the water.

Erik was now standing ready on the logs aft, and when the sea retired he, too, jumped up on to the reef. It was Herman's turn next, and then Bengt's. Each time the raft was pushed a bit farther in, and, when Torstein's turn and my own came, the raft already lay so far in on the reef that there was no longer any ground for abandoning her. All hands began the work of salvage.

We were now twenty yards away from that devilish step up on the reef, and it was there and beyond it that the breakers came rolling after one another in long lines. The coral polyps had taken care to build the atoll so high that only the very tops of the breakers were able to send a fresh stream of sea water past us and into the lagoon, which abounded in fish.

A long way in on the reef the others found the rubber raft, lying drifting and quite waterlogged. They emptied it and dragged it back to the wreck, and we loaded it to the full with the most important equipment, like the radio set, provisions, and water bottles. We dragged all this in across the reef and piled it up on the top of a huge block of coral, which lay alone on the inside of the reef like a large meteorite. Then we went back to the wreck for fresh loads. We could never know what the sea would be up to when the tidal currents got to work around us.

In the shallow water inside the reef we saw something bright shining in the sun. When we waded over to pick it up, to our astonishment we saw two empty tins. This was not exactly what we had expected to find there, and we were still more surprised when we saw that the little boxes were quite bright and newly opened and stamped "Pineapple," with the same inscription as that on the new field rations we ourselves were testing for the quartermaster. They were indeed two of our own pineapple tins which we had thrown over-

We found the dinghy far out on the reef, and used it to carry our equipment ashore.

board after our last meal on board the *Kon-Tiki*. We had followed close behind them up on the reef.

We were standing on sharp, rugged coral blocks, and on the uneven bottom we waded now ankle-deep, now chest-deep, according to the channels and stream beds in the reef.

Where we had stranded, we had only pools of water and wet patches of coral about us; farther in lay the calm blue lagoon. The tide was going out, and we continually saw more corals sticking up out of the water round us, while the surf which thundered without interruption along the reef sank down, as it were, a floor lower. What would happen there on the narrow reef when the tide began to flow again was uncertain. We must get away.

WE FIND AN ISLAND

The reef stretched like a half-submerged fortress wall up to the north and down to the south. In the extreme south was a long island densely covered with tall palm forest. And just above us to the north, only 600 or 700 yards away, lay another but considerably smaller palm island. It lay inside the reef, with palm tops rising into the sky and snow-white sandy beaches running out into the still lagoon. The whole island looked like a bulging green basket of flowers.

This island we chose.

Herman stood beside me beaming all over his bearded face. He did not say a word, only stretched out his hand and laughed quietly. The *Kon-Tiki* still lay far out on the reef with the spray flying over her. She was a wreck, but an honorable wreck. Everything above deck was smashed up, but the nine balsa logs from the Quevedo forest in Ecuador were as intact as ever. They had saved our lives. The sea had claimed but little of the cargo, and none of what we had stowed inside the cabin. We ourselves had stripped the raft of everything of real value, which now lay in safety on the top of the great sun-smitten rock inside the reef.

We had arrived in a new world.

I took a last look round on board the wreck. Johannes had left his hole. He had doubtless found another lurking place here. I caught sight of a little baby palm in a flattened basket. It projected from an eye in a coconut to a length of eighteen inches, and two roots stuck out below. I waded in toward the island with the nut in my hand. A little way ahead I saw Knut wading happily landward with a model of the raft, which he had made with much labor on the voyage, under his arm. We soon passed Bengt. He was a splendid steward. With a lump on his forehead and sea water dripping from his beard, he was walking bent double pushing a box, which danced along before him every time the breakers outside sent a stream over into the lagoon. He lifted the lid proudly. It was the kitchen box, and in it were the primus and cooking utensils in good order.

I shall never forget that wade across the reef toward the heavenly palm island that grew larger as it came to meet us. When I reached the sunny sand beach, I slipped off my shoes and thrust my bare toes down into the warm, bone-dry sand. It was as though I enjoyed the sight of every footprint which dug itself into the virgin sand beach that led up to the palm trunks. Soon the palm tops closed over my head, and I went on, right in toward the center of the tiny island. Green coconuts hung under

A tiny uninhabited island, part of the Raroia atoll, was our first home in the South Seas.

Sunset the first day on our island. It was a curious experience to feel solid ground under our feet again.

the palm tufts, and some luxuriant bushes were thickly covered with snow-white blossoms, which smelled so sweet and seductive that I felt quite faint. In the interior of the island two quite tame terns flew about my shoulders. They were as white and light as wisps of cloud. Small lizards shot away from my feet, and the most important inhabitants of the island were large blood-red hermit crabs which lumbered along in every direction with stolen snail shells as large as eggs adhering to their soft hinder parts.

I was completely overwhelmed. I sank down on my knees and thrust my fingers deep down into the dry warm sand.

The voyage was over. We were all alive. We had run ashore on a small uninhabited South Sea island. And what an island! Torstein came in, flung away a sack, threw himself flat on his back and looked up at the palm tops and the white birds, light as down, which circled noiselessly just above us. Soon we were all six lying there. Herman, always energetic, climbed up a small palm and pulled down a cluster of large green coconuts. We cut off their soft tops with our machete knives, as if they were eggs, and poured down our throats the most delicious refreshing drink in the world—sweet, cold milk from young and seedless palm fruit. On the reef outside resounded the monotonous drum beats from the guard at the gates of paradise.

"Purgatory was a bit damp," said Bengt, "but heaven is more or less as I'd imagined it."

We stretched ourselves luxuriously on the ground and smiled up at the white trade-wind clouds drifting by westward up above the palm tops. Now we were no longer following them helplessly; now we lay on a fixed, motionless island, in Polynesia.

And as we lay and stretched ourselves, the breakers outside us rumbled like a train, to and fro, to and fro, all along the horizon.

Bengt was right; this was heaven.

8. Among Polynesians

OUR LITTLE ISLAND was uninhabited. We soon got to know every palm clump and every beach, for the island was barely two hundred yards across. The highest point was less than six feet above the lagoon.

Over our heads, in the palm tops, there hung great clusters of green coconut husks, which insulated their contents of cold coconut milk from the tropical sun, so we should not be thirsty in the first weeks. There were also ripe coconuts, a swarm of hermit crabs, and all sorts of fish in the lagoon; we should be well off.

On the north side of the island we found the remnants of an old, unpainted wooden cross, half buried in the coral sand. Here there was a view northward along the reef to a stripped wreck, which we had first seen closer in as we drifted by on the way to our stranding. Still farther northward we saw in a bluish haze the palm tufts of another small island. The island to southward, on which the trees grew thickly, was much closer. We saw no sign of life there, either, but for the time we had other matters to think about.

Robinson Crusoe Hesselberg came limping up in his big straw hat with his arms full of crawling hermit crabs. Knut set fire to some dry wood, and soon we had crab and coconut milk with coffee for dessert.

"Feels all right being ashore, doesn't it, boys?" Knut asked delightedly.

He had himself enjoyed this feeling once before on the voyage, at Angatau. As he spoke, he stumbled and poured half a kettle of boiling water over Bengt's bare feet. We were all of us a bit unsteady the first day ashore, after 101 days on board the raft, and would suddenly begin reeling about among the palm trunks be-

Our island was a tropical paradise of waving palms, warm sands, and flowering bushes.

cause we had put out a foot to counter a sea that did not come.

When Bengt handed over to us our respective mess utensils, Erik grinned broadly. I remember that, after the last meal on board, I had leaned over the side of the raft and washed up as usual, while Erik looked in across the reef, saying: "I don't think I shall bother to wash up today." When we found his things in the kitchen box, they were as clean as mine.

After the meal and a good stretch on the ground we set about putting together the soaked radio apparatus; we must do it quickly so that Torstein and Knut might get on the air before the man on Rarotonga sent out a report of our sad end.

Most of the radio equipment had already been brought ashore, and among the things which lay drifting on the reef Bengt found a box, on which he laid hands. He jumped high into the air from an electric shock; there was no doubt that the contents belonged to the radio section. While the operators unscrewed, coupled, and put together, we others set about pitching camp.

Out on the wreck we found the heavy waterlogged sail and dragged it ashore. We stretched it between two big palms in a little opening, looking on to the lagoon, and supported two other corners with bamboo sticks which came drifting in from the wreck. A thick hedge of wild flowering bushes forced the sail together so that we had a roof and three walls and, moreover, a clear view of the shining lagoon, while our nostrils were filled with the sweet scent of blossoms. It was good to be here. We all laughed quietly and enjoyed our ease; we each made our beds of fresh palm leaves, pulling up loose branches of coral which stuck up inconveniently out of the sand. Before night fell we had a very pleasant rest, and over our heads we saw the big bearded face of good old Kon-Tiki. No longer did he swell out his breast with the east wind behind him. He now lay motionless on his back looking up at the stars which came twinkling out over Polynesia.

On the bushes round us hung wet flags and sleeping bags, and soaked articles lay on the sand to dry. Another day on this island of sunshine and everything would be nicely dry. Even the radio boys had to give it up until the sun had a chance of drying the inside of their apparatus next day. We took the sleeping bags down from the trees and turned in, disputing boastfully as to who had the driest bag. Bengt won, for his did not squelch when he turned over. Heavens, how good it was to be able to sleep!

When we woke next morning at sunrise, the sail was bent down and full of rain water as pure as crystal. Bengt took charge of this asset and then ambled down to the lagoon and jerked ashore some curious breakfast fish which he decoyed into channels in the sand.

That night Herman had had pains in the neck and back where he had injured himself before the start from Lima, and Erik had a return of his vanished lumbago. Otherwise we had come out of the trip over the reef astonishingly lightly, with scratches, small wounds, and Bengt's slight concussion. I myself looked most peculiar, with my arms and legs bruised blue black all over by the pressure against the rope.

But none of us was in such a bad state that the sparkling clear lagoon did not entice him to a brisk swim before breakfast. The bitter salt water was so pure and clear that gaily colored corals in nine feet of water seemed so near the surface that we thought we should cut our toes on them in swimming. And the water abounded in beautiful varieties of colorful fish. The water was just cold enough to be refreshing, and the air was pleasantly warm and dry from the sun. But we must get ashore again quickly today; Rarotonga would broadcast alarming news if nothing had been heard from the raft at the end of the day.

THE RADIO CRISIS

Coils and radio parts lay drying in the tropical sun on slabs of coral, and Torstein and Knut coupled and screwed. The whole day passed, and the atmosphere grew more and more hectic. The rest of us abandoned all other jobs and crowded round the radio in the hope of being able to give assistance. We must be on the air before 10 P.M. Then the thirty-six hours' time limit would be up, and the radio amateur on Rarotonga would send out appeals for airplane and relief expeditions.

Noon came, afternoon came, and the sun set. If only the man on Rarotonga would contain himself! Seven o'clock, eight, nine. The tension was at breaking point. Not a sign of life in the transmitter, but the receiver, an NC–173, began to liven up somewhere at the bottom of the scale and we heard faint music. But not on the amateur wave length. It was eating its way up, however; perhaps it was a wet coil which was drying inward from one end. The transmitter was still stone-dead— short circuits and sparks everywhere.

There was less than an hour left. This would never do. The regular transmitter was given up, and a little sabotage transmitter from wartime was tried again. We had tested it several times before in the course of the day, but without result. Now perhaps it had become a little drier. All the batteries were completely ruined, and we got power by cranking a tiny hand generator. It was heavy, and we four who were laymen in radio matters took turns all day long sitting and turning the infernal thing.

The thirty-six hours would soon be up. I remember someone whispering, "Seven minutes more," "Five minutes more," and then no one would look at his watch again. The transmitter was as dumb as ever, but the receiver was sputtering upward toward the right wave length. Suddenly it crackled on the Rarotonga man's frequency, and we gathered that he was in full contact with the telegraph station in Tahiti. Soon afterward we picked up the following fragment of a message sent out from Rarotonga:

" - - - no plane this side of Samoa. I am quite sure - - -"

Then it died away again. The tension was unbearable. What was brewing out there? Had they already begun to send out plane and rescue expeditions? Now, no doubt, messages concerning us were going over the air in every direction.

The two operators worked feverishly. The sweat trickled from their faces as freely as it

For hours, Erik and Knut struggled to send out a radio message that would notify our friends we were safe and no rescue was necessary.

did from ours who sat turning the handle. Power began slowly to come into the transmitter's aerial, and Torstein pointed ecstatically to an arrow which swung slowly up over a scale when he held the Morse key down. Now it was coming!

We turned the handle madly while Torstein called Rarotonga. No one heard us. Once more. Now the receiver was working again, but Rarotonga did not hear us. We called Hal and Frank at Los Angeles and the Naval School at Lima, but no one heard us.

Then Torstein sent out a CQ message: that is to say, he called all the stations in the world which could hear us on our special amateur wave length.

That was of some use. Now a faint voice out in the ether began to call us slowly. We called again and said that we heard him. Then the slow voice out in the ether said:

"My name is Paul—I live in Colorado. What is your name and where do you live?"

This was a radio amateur. Torstein seized the key, while we turned the handle, and replied:

"This is the *Kon-Tiki*. We are stranded on desert island in the Pacific."

Paul did not believe the message. He

On the beach we planted one of the coconuts we had carried across the Pacific from Peru.

thought it was a radio amateur in the next street pulling his leg, and he did not come on the air again. We tore our hair in desperation. Here were we, sitting under the palm tops on a starry night on a desert island, and no one even believed what we said.

Torstein did not give up; he was at the key again sending "All well, all well, all well" unceasingly. We must at all costs stop all this rescue machinery from starting out across the Pacific.

Then we heard, rather faintly, in the receiver:

"If all's well, why worry?"

Then all was quiet in the ether. That was all.

We could have leaped into the air and shaken down all the coconuts for sheer desperation, and heaven knows what we should have done if both Rarotonga and good old Hal had not suddenly heard us. Hal wept for delight, he said, at hearing LI 2 B again. All the tension stopped immediately; we were once more alone and undisturbed on our South Sea island and turned in, worn out, on our beds of palm leaves.

Next day we took it easy and enjoyed life to the full. Some bathed, others fished or went exploring on the reef in search of curious marine creatures, while the most energetic cleared up in camp and made our surroundings pleasant. Out on the point which looked toward the *Kon-Tiki* we dug a hole on the edge of the trees, lined it with leaves, and planted in it the sprouting coconut from Peru. A cairn of corals was erected beside it, opposite the place where the *Kon-Tiki* had run ashore.

The *Kon-Tiki* had been washed still farther in during the night and lay almost dry in a few pools of water, squeezed in among a group of big coral blocks a long way through the reef.

After a thorough baking in the warm sand, Erik and Herman were in fine fettle again and were anxious to go southward along the reef in the hope of getting over to the large island which lay down there. I warned them more against eels than against sharks, and each of them stuck his long machete knife into his belt. I knew the coral reef was the habitat of a frightful eel with long poisonous teeth which could easily tear off a man's leg. They wriggle to the attack with lightning rapidity and are the terror of the natives, who are not afraid to swim round a shark.

The two men were able to wade over long stretches of the reef to southward, but there were occasional channels of deeper water running this way and that where they had to jump in and swim. They reached the big island safely and waded ashore. The island, long and narrow and covered with palm forest, ran farther south between sunny beaches under the shelter of the reef. The two continued along the island till they came to the southern point.

From here the reef, covered with white foam, ran on southward to other distant islands. They found the wreck of a big ship down there; she had four masts and lay on the shore cut in two. She was an old Spanish sailing vessel which had been loaded with rails, and rusty rails lay scattered all along the reef. They returned along the other side of the island but did not find so much as a track in the sand.

UNINHABITED ISLANDS

Our existence on the island was heavenly, but we could not spend all our lives here, and we must begin to think about how we should get back to the outer world. After a week the *Kon-Tiki* had bumped her way in to the middle of the reef, where she lay stuck fast on dry land. The great logs had pushed away and broken off large slabs of coral in the effort to force their way forward to the lagoon, but now the wooden raft lay immovable, and all our pulling and all our pushing were useless. If we could only get the wreck into the la-

The forms of coral found in a coral reef are beautifully varied in shape and color. The reefs are built by tiny living polyps over centuries of time.

goon, we could always splice the mast and rig her sufficiently to be able to sail with the wind across the friendly lagoon and see what we found on the other side. If any of the islands were inhabited, it must be some of those which lay along the horizon away in the west, where the atoll turned its face toward the lee side.

The days passed.

Then one morning some of the fellows came tearing up and said they had seen a white sail on the lagoon. From up among the palm trunks we could see a tiny speck which was curiously white against the opal-blue lagoon. It was evidently a sail close to land on the other side. We could see that it was tacking. Soon another appeared.

They grew in size, as the morning went on, and came nearer. They came straight toward us. We hoisted the French flag on a palm tree and waved our own Norwegian flag on a pole. One of the sails was now so near that we could see that it belonged to a Polynesian outrigger canoe. The rig was of more recent type. Two brown figures stood on board gazing at us. We waved. They waved back and sailed straight in on to the shallows.

"*Ia-ora-na*," we greeted them in Polynesian.

"*Ia-ora-na*," they shouted back in chorus, and one jumped out and dragged his canoe after him as he came wading over the sandy shallows straight toward us.

The two men had white men's clothes but brown men's bodies. They were barelegged, well built, and wore homemade straw hats to protect them from the sun. They landed and approached us rather uncertainly, but when we smiled and shook hands with them in turn, they beamed on us with rows of pearly teeth which said more than words.

Our Polynesian greeting had astonished and encouraged the two canoers in exactly the same way as we ourselves had been deceived when their kinsman off Angatau had called out "Good night," and they reeled off a long rhapsody in Polynesian before they realized that their outpourings were going wide of the mark. Then they had nothing more to say but giggled amiably and pointed to the other canoe which was approaching.

There were three men in this, and, when they waded ashore and greeted us, it appeared that one of them could talk a little French. We learned that there was a native village on one of the islands across the lagoon, and from it the Polynesians had seen our fire several nights earlier. Now there was only one passage leading in through the Raroia reef to the circle of islands around the lagoon, and, as this passage ran right past the village, no one could approach these islands inside the reef without being seen by the inhabitants of the village. The old people in the village, therefore, had come to the conclusion that the light they saw on the reef to eastward could not be the work of men but must be something supernatural. This had quenched in them all desire to go across and see for themselves. But then part of a box had come drifting across the lagoon, and on it some signs were painted. Two of the natives, who had been on Tahiti and learned the alphabet, had deciphered the inscription and read TIKI in big black letters on the slab of wood. Then there was no longer any doubt that there were ghosts on the reef, for Tiki was the long-dead founder of their own race—they all knew that. But then tinned bread, cigarettes, cocoa, and a box with an old shoe in it came drifting across the lagoon. Now they all realized that there had been a shipwreck on the eastern side of the reef, and the chief sent out two canoes to search for the survivors whose fire they had seen on the island.

Urged on by the others, the brown man who spoke French asked why the slab of wood that drifted across the lagoon had "Tiki" on it. We explained that "Kon-Tiki" was on all our equipment and that it was the name of the vessel in which we had come.

Our new friends were loud in their astonishment when they heard that all on board had been saved, when the vessel stranded, and that the flattened wreck out on the reef was actually the craft in which we had come. They wanted to put us all into the canoes at once and take us across to the village. We thanked them and refused, as we wanted to stay till we had got the *Kon-Tiki* off the reef. They looked aghast at the flat contraption out on

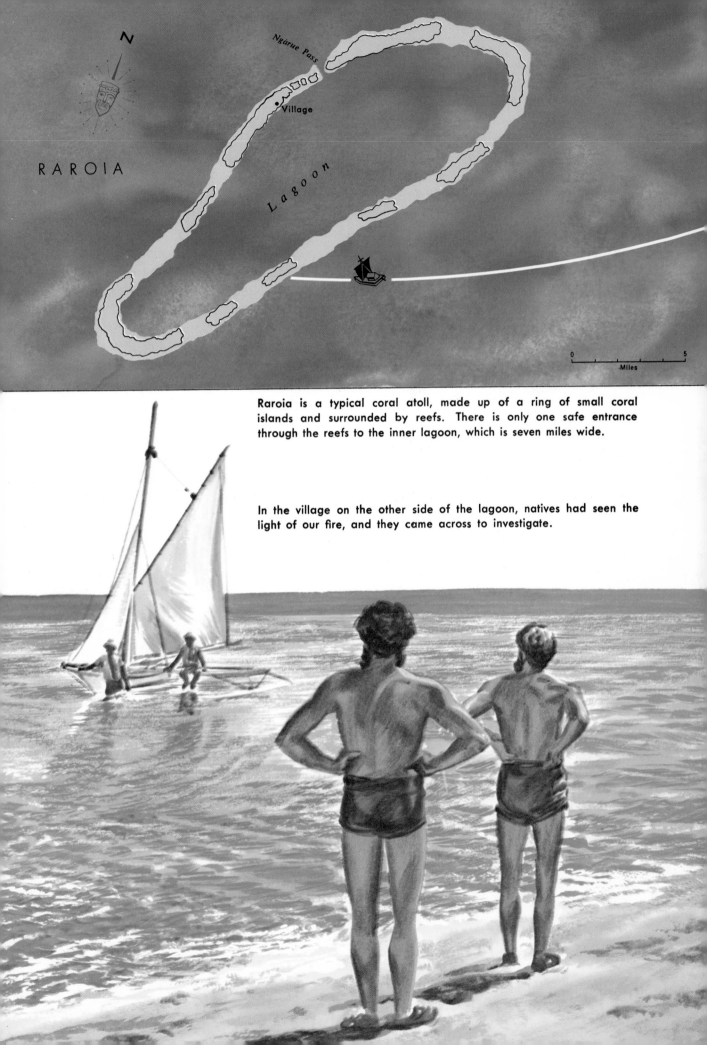

N

Ngārue Pass

Village

RAROIA

Lagoon

0   5
·Miles

Raroia is a typical coral atoll, made up of a ring of small coral islands and surrounded by reefs. There is only one safe entrance through the reefs to the inner lagoon, which is seven miles wide.

In the village on the other side of the lagoon, natives had seen the light of our fire, and they came across to investigate.

the reef; surely we could not dream of getting that collapsed hull afloat again! Finally the spokesman said emphatically that we must go with them; the chief had given them strict orders not to return without us.

We then decided that one of us should go with the natives as envoy to the chief and should then come back and report to us on the conditions on the other island. We would not let the raft remain on the reef and could not abandon all the equipment on our little island. Bengt went with the natives. The two canoes were pushed off from the sand and soon disappeared westward with a fair wind.

Next day the horizon swarmed with white sails. Now, it seemed, the natives were coming to fetch us with all the craft they had.

THE CHIEF VISITS US

The whole convoy tacked across toward us, and, when they came near, we saw our good friend Bengt waving his hat in the first canoe, surrounded by brown figures. He shouted to us that the chief himself was with him, and the five of us formed up respectfully down on the beach where they were wading ashore.

Chief Teka of Raroia came in person to invite us to visit the village across the lagoon.

Bengt presented us to the chief with great ceremony. The chief's name, Bengt said, was Tepiuraiarii Teriifaatau, but he would understand whom we meant if we called him Teka. We called him Teka.

Teka was a tall, slender Polynesian with uncommonly intelligent eyes. He was an important person, a descendant of the old royal line in Tahiti, and was chief of both the Raroia and the Takume islands. He had been to school in Tahiti, so that he spoke French and could both read and write. He told me that the capital of Norway was called Christiania and asked if I knew Bing Crosby. He also told us that only three foreign vessels had called at Raroia in the last ten years, but that the village was visited several times a year by the native copra schooner from Tahiti, which brought merchandise and took away coconut kernels in exchange. They had been expecting the schooner for some weeks now, so she might come at any time.

Bengt's report, summarized, was that there was no school, radio, or any white men on Raroia, but that the 127 Polynesians in the village had done all they could to make us comfortable there and had prepared a great reception for us when we came over.

The chief's first request was to see the boat which had brought us ashore on the reef alive. We waded out toward the *Kon-Tiki* with a string of natives after us. When we drew near, the natives suddenly stopped and uttered loud exclamations, all talking at once. We could now see the logs of the *Kon-Tiki* plainly, and one of the natives burst out:

"That's not a boat, it's a *pae-pae!*"

"*Pae-pae!*" they all repeated in chorus.

They splashed out across the reef at a gallop and clambered up on to the *Kon-Tiki*. They scrambled about everywhere like excited children, feeling the logs, the bamboo plaiting, and the ropes. The chief was in as high spirits as the others; he came back and repeated with an inquiring expression:

"The *Tiki* isn't a boat, she's a *pae-pae*."

Pae-pae is the Polynesian word for "raft" and "platform," and on Easter Island it is also the word used for the natives' canoes. The chief told us that such *pae-pae* no longer existed, but that the oldest men in the village could relate old traditions of them. The natives all outshouted one another in admiration for the great balsa logs, but they turned up their noses at the ropes. Ropes like that did not last many months in salt water and sun. They showed us with pride the lashings on their own outriggers; they had plaited them themselves of coconut hemp, and such ropes remained as good as new for five years at sea.

When we waded back to our little island, it was named Fenua Kon-Tiki, or Kon-Tiki Island. This was a name we could all pronounce, but our brown friends had a hard job trying to pronounce our short Christian names. They were delighted when I said they could call me Terai Mateata, for the great chief in Tahiti had given me that name when adopting me as his "son" the first time I was in those parts.

The natives brought out fowls and eggs and breadfruit from the canoes, while others speared big fish in the lagoon with three-pronged spears, and we had a feast round the campfire. We had to narrate all our experiences with the *pae-pae* at sea, and they wanted to hear about the whale shark again and again. And every time we came to the point at which Erik rammed the harpoon into its skull, they uttered the same cries of excitement. They recognized at once every single fish of which we showed them sketches and promptly gave us the names in Polynesian. But they had never seen or heard of the whale shark or the snake mackerel.

When the evening came, we turned on the radio, to the great delight of the whole assemblage. Church music was most to their taste until, to our own astonishment, we picked up real hula music from America. Then the liveliest of them began to wriggle with their arms curved over their heads, and soon the whole company sprang up on their haunches and danced the hula-hula in time with the music. When night came, all camped round a fire on

The natives were expert at spearing fish with their three-pronged spears.

the beach. It was as much of an adventure to the natives as it was to us.

When we awoke next morning, they were already up and frying newly caught fish, while six freshly opened coconut shells stood ready for us to quench our morning thirst.

The reef was thundering more than usual that day; the wind had increased in strength, and the surf was whipping high into the air out there behind the wreck.

"The *Tiki* will come in today," said the chief, pointing to the wreck. "There'll be a high tide."

KON-TIKI IS SAFE

About eleven o'clock the water began to flow past us into the lagoon. The lagoon began to fill like a big basin, and the water rose all round the island. Later in the day the real inflow from the sea came. The water came rolling in, terrace after terrace, and more and more of the reef sank below the surface of the sea. The masses of water rolled forward along both sides of the island. They tore away large coral blocks and dug up great sandbanks which disappeared like flour before the wind, while others were built up. Loose bamboos from the wreck came sailing past us, and the *Kon-Tiki* began to move. Everything that was lying along the beach had to be carried up into the interior of the island so that it might not be caught by the tide. Soon only the highest stones on the reef were visible, and all the beaches round our island had gone, while the water flowed up toward the herbage of the pancake island. This was eerie. It looked as if the whole sea were invading us. The *Kon-Tiki* swung right round and drifted until she was caught by some other coral blocks.

The natives flung themselves into the water and swam and waded through the eddies till, moving from bank to bank, they reached the raft. Knut and Erik followed. Ropes lay ready on board the raft, and, when she rolled over the last coral blocks and broke loose from the reef, the natives jumped overboard and tried to hold her. They did not know the *Kon-Tiki* and her ungovernable urge to push on westward; so they were towed along helplessly

with her. She was soon moving at a good speed right across the reef and into the lagoon. She became slightly at a loss when she reached quieter water and seemed to be looking round as though to obtain a survey of further possibilities. Before she began to move again and discovered the exit across the lagoon, the natives had already succeeded in getting the end of the rope around a palm on land. And there the *Kon-Tiki* hung, tied up fast in the lagoon. The craft that went over land and water had made her way across the barricade and into the lagoon in the interior of Raroia.

With inspiring war cries, to which "*ke-ke-te-huru-huru*" formed an animating refrain, we hauled the *Kon-Tiki* by our combined efforts in to the shore of the island of her own name. The tide reached a point four feet above normal high water. We had thought the whole island was going to disappear before our eyes.

The wind-whipped waves were breaking all over the lagoon, and we could not get much of our equipment into the narrow, wet canoes. The natives had to get back to the village in a hurry, and Bengt and Herman went with them to see a small boy who lay dying in a hut in the village. The boy had an abscess on his head, and we had penicillin.

Next day we four were alone on Kon-Tiki Island. The east wind was now so strong that the natives could not come across the lagoon, which was studded with sharp coral formations and shoals. The tide, which had somewhat receded, flowed in again fiercely, in long, rushing step formations.

Next day it was quieter again. We were now able to dive under the *Kon-Tiki* and ascertain that the nine logs were intact, even if the reef had planed an inch or two off the bottom. The cordage lay so deep in its grooves that only four of the numerous ropes had been cut by the corals. We set about clearing up on board. Our proud vessel looked better when the mess had been removed from the deck, the cabin pulled out again like a concertina, and the mast spliced and set upright.

NATIVES COME FOR US

In the course of the day the sails appeared on the horizon again; the natives were coming

Repairing the rescued raft. After clearing the deck, we straightened the cabin and spliced the mast.

After a high tide had freed the *Kon-Tiki* from the reef, the natives towed it into the lagoon.

to fetch us and the rest of the cargo. Herman and Bengt were with them, and they told us that the natives had prepared great festivities in the village. When we got over to the other island, we must not leave the canoes till the chief himself had indicated that we might do so.

We ran across the lagoon, which here was seven miles wide, before a fresh breeze. It was with real sorrow that we saw the familiar palms on Kon-Tiki Island waving us good-by as they changed into a clump and shrank into one small indefinable island like all the others along the eastern reef. But ahead of us larger islands were broadening out. And on one of them we saw a jetty and smoke rising from huts among the palm trunks.

The village looked quite dead; not a soul was to be seen. What was brewing now? Down on the beach, behind a jetty of coral blocks, stood two solitary figures, one tall and thin and one big and stout as a barrel. As we came in, we saluted them both. They were the chief Teka and the vice-chief Tupuhoe. We all fell for Tupuhoe's broad hearty smile. Teka was a clear brain and a diplomat, but Tupuhoe was a pure child of nature and a sterling fellow, with a humor and a primitive force the like of which one meets but rarely. With his powerful body and kingly features he was exactly what one expects a Polynesian chief to be. Tupuhoe was, indeed, the real chief on the island, but Teka had gradually acquired the supreme position because he could speak

Vice-chief Tupuhoe had all the kingly qualities of a true Polynesian chief.

serious; even our cheerful friends from Kon-Tiki Island stood drawn up among the others and did not give us a sign of recognition.

RECEPTION IN THE VILLAGE

When we had all come out on the steps, the whole assembly opened their mouths simultaneously and joined in singing—the "Marseillaise"! Teka, who knew the words, led the singing, and it went fairly well in spite of a few old women getting stuck up on the high notes. They had been training hard for this. The French and Norwegian flags were hoisted in front of the steps, and this ended the official reception by the chief Teka. He retired quietly into the background, and now stout Tupuhoe sprang forward and became master of the ceremonies. Tupuhoe gave a quick sign, on which the whole assembly burst into a new song. This time it went better, for the tune was composed by themselves and the words, too, were in their language—and sing their own hula they could. The melody was so fascinating, in all its touching simplicity, that we felt a tingling down our backs as the South Sea came roaring toward us. A few individuals led the singing and the whole choir joined in regularly; there were variations in the melody, though the words were always the same:

"Good day, Terai Mateata and your men, who have come across the sea on a *pae-pae* to us on Raroia; yes, good day, may you remain long among us and share memories with us so that we can always be together, even when you go away to a far land. Good day."

We had to ask them to sing the song over again, and more and more life came into the whole assembly as they began to feel less constrained. Then Tupuhoe asked me to say a few words to the people as to why we had come across the sea on a *pae-pae;* they had all been counting on this. I was to speak in French, and Teka would translate bit by bit.

It was an uneducated but highly intelligent gathering of brown people that stood waiting for me to speak. I told them that I had been among their kinsmen out here in the South Sea islands before, and that I had heard of their first chief, Tiki, who had brought their

French and count and write, so that the village was not cheated when the schooner came from Tahiti to fetch copra.

Teka explained that we were to march together up to the meetinghouse in the village, and when all the boys had come ashore we set off thither in ceremonial procession, Herman first with the flag waving on a harpoon shaft, and then I myself between the two chiefs.

The village bore obvious marks of the copra trade with Tahiti; both planks and corrugated iron had been imported in the schooner. While some huts were built in a picturesque old-fashioned style, with twigs and plaited palm leaves, others were knocked together with nails and planks as small tropical bungalows. A large house built of planks, standing alone among the palms, was the new village meetinghouse; there we six whites were to stay. We marched in with the flag by a small back door and out on to a broad flight of steps before the façade. Before us in the square stood everyone in the village who could walk or crawl—women and children, old and young. All were intensely

The native houses on Raroia were a mixture of old and modern. Some were palm-thatched huts; other looked like tropical bungalows.

forefathers out to the islands from a mysterious country whose whereabouts no one knew any longer. But in a distant land called Peru, I said, a mighty chief had once ruled whose name was Tiki. The people called him Kon-Tiki, or Sun-Tiki, because he said he was descended from the sun. Tiki and a number of followers had at last disappeared from their country on big *pae-paes*; therefore we six thought that he was the same Tiki who had come to those islands. As nobody would believe that a *pae-pae* could make the voyage across the sea, we ourselves had set out from Peru on a *pae-pae*, and here we were, so it could be done.

When the little speech was translated by Teka, Tupuhoe was all fire and flame and sprang forward in front of the assembly in a kind of ecstasy. He rumbled away in Polynesian, flung out his arms, pointed to heaven and us, and in his flood of speech constantly repeated the word Tiki. He talked so fast that it was impossible to follow the thread of what

he said, but the whole assembly swallowed every word and was visibly excited. Teka, on the contrary, looked quite embarrassed when he had to translate.

Tupuhoe had said that his father and grandfather, and his fathers before him, had told of Tiki and had said that Tiki was their first chief who was now in heaven. Now we six had come to them across the sea on a *pae-pae*. We were the first whites who had admitted that their fathers had spoken the truth. Tiki had lived, he had been real, but now he was dead and in heaven.

Three old men pushed forward and wanted to shake hands with us. There was no doubt that it was they who had kept the memories of Tiki alive among the people, and the chief told us that one of the old men knew an immense number of traditions and historical ballads from his forefathers' time. I asked the old man if there was, in the traditions, any hint of the direction from which Tiki had come.

153

No, none of the old men could remember having heard that. But after long and careful reflection the oldest of the three said that Tiki had with him a near relation who was called Maui, and in the ballad of Maui it was said that he had come to the islands from Pura and *pura* was the word for the part of the sky where the sun rose. If Maui had come from Pura, the old man said, Tiki had no doubt come from the same place, and we six on the *pae-pae* had also come from *pura*—that was sure enough.

I told the brown men that on a lonely island near Easter Island, called Mangareva, the people had never learned the use of canoes and had continued to use big *pae-paes* at sea right down to our time. This the old men did not know, but they knew that their forefathers also had used big *pae-paes*. However, they had gradually gone out of use, and now they had nothing but the name and traditions left.

Now the whole village was allowed to come up and shake hands with each of us. The men mumbled "*ia-ora-na*" and almost shook our hands out of joint, while the girls squirmed forward and greeted us coquettishly yet shyly and the old women babbled and cackled and pointed to our beards and the color of our skin. Friendliness beamed from every face, so it was quite immaterial that there was a hubbub of linguistic confusion. If they said something incomprehensible to us in Polynesian, we gave them tit for tat in Norwegian. We had the greatest fun together. The first native word we all learned was the word for "like," and when, moreover, one could point to what one liked and count on getting it at once, it was all very simple. If one wrinkled one's nose when "like" was said, it meant "don't like," and on this basis we got along pretty well.

HULA FEAST

As soon as we had become acquainted with the 127 inhabitants of the village, a long table was laid for the two chiefs and the six of us, and the village girls came round bearing the most delicious dishes. While some arranged the table, others came and hung plaited wreaths of flowers round our necks and smaller wreaths round our heads. These exhaled a lingering scent and were cool and refreshing in the heat. And so a feast of welcome began which did not end till we left the island weeks after. Our eyes opened wide and our mouths watered, for the tables were loaded with roast suckling pigs, chickens, roast ducks, fresh lobsters, Polynesian fish dishes, breadfruit, papaya, and coconut milk. While we attacked the dishes, we were entertained by the crowd singing hula songs, while young girls danced round the table.

The boys laughed and thoroughly enjoyed themselves, each of us looking more absurd than the next as we sat and gorged like starving men, with flowing beards and wreaths of flowers in our hair. The two chiefs were enjoying life as wholeheartedly as ourselves.

After the meal there was hula dancing on a grand scale. The village wanted to show us their local folk dances. While we six and Teka and Tupuhoe were each given stools in the orchestra, two guitar players advanced, squatted down, and began to strum real South Sea melodies. Two ranks of dancing men and women, with rustling skirts of palm leaves round their hips, came gliding and wriggling forward through the ring of spectators who squatted and sang. At first the dancers seemed a little self-conscious and nervous, but when they saw that the white men from the *pae-pae* did not turn up their noses at their ancestors' folk dances, the dancing became more and more animated. Some of the older people joined in; they had a splendid rhythm and could dance dances which were obviously no longer in common use. As the sun sank into the Pacific, the dancing under the palm trees became livelier and livelier, and the applause of the spectators more and more spontaneous. They had forgotten that we who sat watching them were six strangers; we were now six of their own people, enjoying ourselves with them.

The repertory was endless; one fascinating display followed another. Finally a crowd of young men squatted down in a close ring just

After a mouth-watering feast, our new friends entertained us with a fascinating display of native dances.

A guitar-strumming youth and graceful hula girl of the South Seas.

in front of us, and at a sign from Tupuhoe they began to beat time rhythmically on the ground with the palms of their hands. First slowly, then more quickly, and the rhythm grew more and more perfect when a drummer suddenly joined in and accompanied them, beating at a furious pace with two sticks on a bone-dry, hollowed block of wood which emitted a sharp, intense sound. When the rhythm reached the desired degree of animation, the singing began, and suddenly a hula girl with a wreath of flowers round her neck and flowers behind one ear leaped into the ring. She kept time to the music with bare feet and bent knees, swaying rhythmically at the hips and curving her arms above her head in true Polynesian style. She danced splendidly, and soon the whole assembly were beating time with their hands. Another girl leaped into the ring, and after her another. They moved

with incredible suppleness in perfect rhythm, gliding round one another in the dance like graceful shadows. The dull beating of hands on the ground, the singing, and the cheerful wooden drum increased their tempo faster and faster and the dance grew wilder and wilder, while the spectators howled and clapped in perfect rhythm.

This was the South Seas life as the old days had known it. The stars twinkled and the palms waved. The night was mild and long and full of the scent of flowers and the song of crickets. Tupuhoe beamed and slapped me on the shoulder.

Even Teka thought it was a very good feast; it was the first time white men had been present at their dances on Raroia, he said. Faster and faster, faster and faster, went the rolls of the drums, the clapping, singing, and dancing.

To the boundless delight of the crowd Herman sprang into the ring and, half crouching, tackled all the difficult wriggling movements of the hula. The jubilation was unbounded. Soon Bengt and Torstein leaped into the dance, striving till the perspiration streamed down their faces to keep up with the tempo, which rose and rose to a furious pace till the drum alone was beating in one prolonged drone and the three real hula dancers quivering in time like aspen leaves. Then they sank down in the finales and the drumbeats ceased abruptly.

Now the evening was ours. There was no end to the enthusiasm.

The next item on the program was the bird dance, which was one of the oldest ceremonies on Raroia. Men and women in two ranks jumped forward in a rhythmic dance, imitating flocks of birds following a leader. The dance leader had the title of chief of the birds and performed curious maneuvers without actually joining in the dance. When the dance was over, Tupuhoe explained that it had been performed in honor of the raft and would now be repeated, but the dance leader would be relieved by myself. As the dance leader's main task appeared to me to consist in uttering wild howls, hopping around on his haunches, wriggling his backside, and waving his hands over his head, I pulled the wreath of flowers well down over my head and marched out into the arena. While I was curving myself in the dance, I saw old Tupuhoe laughing till he nearly fell off his stool, and the music grew feeble because the singers and players followed Tupuhoe's example.

Now everyone wanted to dance, old and young alike, and soon the drummer and earth-beaters were there again, giving the lead to a fiery hula-hula dance. First the hula girls sprang into the ring and started the dance at a tempo that grew wilder and wilder, and then we were invited to dance in turn, while more and more men and women followed, stamping and writhing along, faster and faster.

The feast went on till broad daylight, when we were allowed to have a little pause, after again shaking hands with every one of the 127. We shook hands with every one of them every morning and every evening throughout our stay on the island. Six beds were scraped together from all the huts in the village and placed side by side along the wall in the meetinghouse, and in these we slept in a row like the seven little dwarfs in the fairy story, with sweet-smelling wreaths of flowers hanging above our heads.

Next day the boy of six who had an abscess on his head seemed to be in a bad way. He had a temperature of 106°, and the abscess was as large as a man's fist and throbbed painfully.

Teka declared that they had lost a number of children in this way and that, if none of us could do any doctoring, the boy had not many days to live. We had bottles of penicillin in a new tablet form, but we did not know what dose a small child could stand. If the boy died under our treatment, it might have serious consequences for all of us.

MEDICINE MEN ON THE AIR

Knut and Torstein got the radio out again and slung up an aerial between the tallest coconut palms. When evening came they got in touch again with our unseen friends, Hal and Frank, sitting in their rooms at home in Los Angeles. Frank called a doctor on the telephone, and we signaled with the Morse key all the boy's symptoms and a list of what we had available in our medical chest. Frank passed on the doctor's reply, and that night we went off to the hut where little Haumata lay tossing in a fever with half the village weeping and making a noise about him.

Herman and Knut were to do the doctoring, while we others had more than enough to do to keep the villagers outside. The mother became hysterical when we came with a sharp knife and asked for boiling water. It was a grave moment. When the abscess was drained and sterilized, the boy's head was bound up and we began the penicillin cure. For two days and nights, while the fever was at its maximum, the boy was treated every four hours, and the abscess was kept open. And each evening the doctor in Los Angeles was consulted. Then the boy's temperature fell suddenly, the

pus was replaced by plasma which was allowed to heal, and the boy was beaming and wanting to look at pictures from the white man's strange world.

A week later Haumata was playing on the beach with the other children, his head bound up in a big bandage.

When this had gone well, there was no end to the maladies which cropped up in the village. Toothache and gastric troubles were everywhere, and both old and young had boils in one place or another. We referred the patients to Dr. Knut and Dr. Herman, who ordered diets and emptied the medicine chest of pills and ointments.

WE BECOME ROYALTY

We had not been among our brown admirers for many days before the festivities culminated in a fresh ceremony. We were to be adopted as citizens of Raroia and receive Polynesian names. I myself was no longer to be Terai Mateata; I could be called that in Tahiti, but not here among them.

Six stools were placed for us in the middle of the square, and the whole village was out early to get good places in the circle. Teka sat solemnly among them; he was chief all right, but not where old local ceremonies were concerned. Then Tupuhoe took over.

All sat waiting, silent and profoundly serious, while portly Tupuhoe approached solemnly and slowly with his stout knotted stick. He was conscious of the gravity of the moment, and the eyes of all were upon him as he **came up, deep in thought, and took up his** position in front of us. He was the born chief —a brilliant speaker and actor.

He turned to the chief singers, drummers, and dance leaders, pointed at them in turn with his knotted stick, and gave them curt orders in low, measured tones. Then he turned to us again, and suddenly opened his great eyes wide, so that the large white eyeballs shone as bright as the teeth in his expressive copper-brown face. He raised the knotted stick and, the words streaming from his lips in an un-

interrupted flow, he recited ancient rituals which none but the oldest members understood, because they were in an old forgotten dialect.

Then he told us, with Teka as interpreter, that Tikaroa was the name of the first king who had established himself on the island, and that he had reigned over this same atoll from north to south, from east to west, and up into the sky above men's heads.

While the whole choir joined in the old ballad about King Tikaroa, Tupuhoe laid his great hand on my chest and, turning to the audience, said that he was naming me Varoa Tikaroa, or Tikaroa's Spirit.

When the song died away, it was the turn of Herman and Bengt. They had the big brown hand laid upon their chests in turn and received the names Tupuhoe-Itetahua and Topakino. These were the names of two old-time heroes who had fought a savage sea monster and killed it at the entrance to the Raroia reef.

The drummer delivered a few vigorous rolls, and two robust men with knotted-up loincloths and a long spear in each hand sprang forward. They broke into a march in double-quick time, with their knees raised to their chests and their spears pointing upward, and turned their heads from side to side. At a fresh beat of the drum they leaped into the air and, in perfect rhythm, began a ceremonial battle in the purest ballet style. The whole thing was short and swift and represented the heroes' fight with the sea monster. Then Torstein was named with song and ceremony; he was called **Maroake**, after a former king in the present village, and Erik and Knut received the names of Tane-Matarau and Tefaunui after two navigators and sea heroes of the past. The long monotonous recitation which accompanied their naming was delivered at breakneck speed and with a continuous flow of words, the incredible rapidity of which was calculated both to impress and amuse.

The ceremony was over. Once more there were white and bearded chiefs among the Polynesian people on Raroia. Two ranks of male and female dancers came forward in plaited straw skirts with swaying bast crowns on their

The author in native dress with two young friends.

heads. They danced forward to us and transferred the crowns from their own heads to ours; we had rustling straw skirts put round our waists, and the festivities continued.

One night the flower-clad radio operators got into touch with the radio amateur on Rarotonga, who passed on a message to us from Tahiti. It was a cordial welcome from the governor of the French Pacific colonies.

On instructions from Paris he had sent the government schooner *Tamara* to fetch us to Tahiti, so we should not have to wait for the uncertain arrival of the copra schooner. Tahiti was the central point of the French colonies and the only island which had contact with the world in general. We should have to go via Tahiti to get the regular boat home to our own world.

The festivities continued on Raroia. One night some strange hoots were heard from out at sea, and lookout men came down from the palm tops and reported that a vessel was lying at the entrance to the lagoon. We ran through the palm forest and down to the beach on the lee side. Here we looked out over the sea in the opposite direction to that from which we had come. There were much smaller breakers on this side, which lay under the shelter of the entire atoll and the reef.

ANOTHER SHIPWRECK

Just outside the entrance to the lagoon we saw the lights of a vessel. Since the night was clear and starry, we could distinguish the outlines of a broad-beamed schooner with two masts. Was this the governor's ship which was coming for us? Why did she not come in?

The natives grew more and more uneasy. Now we too saw what was happening. The vessel had a heavy list and threatened to capsize. She was aground on an invisible coral reef under the surface.

Torstein got hold of a light and signaled: *"Quel bateau?"*

"Maoae," was flashed back.

The *Maoae* was the copra schooner which ran between the islands. She was on her way to Raroia to fetch copra. There was a Polynesian captain and crew on board, and

they knew the reefs inside out. But the current out of the lagoon was treacherous in darkness. It was lucky that the schooner lay under the lee of the island and that the weather was quiet. The list of the *Maoae* became heavier and heavier, and the crew took to the boat. Strong ropes were made fast to her mastheads and rowed in to the land, where the natives fastened them round coconut palms to prevent the schooner from capsizing. The crew, with other ropes, stationed themselves off the opening in the reef in their boat, in the hope of rowing the *Maoae* off when the tidal current ran out of the lagoon. The people of the village launched all their canoes and set out to salvage the cargo. There were ninety tons of valuable copra on board. Load after load of sacks of copra was transferred from the rolling schooner and brought on to dry land.

At high water the *Maoae* was still aground, bumping and rolling against the corals until she sprang a leak. When day broke she was lying in a worse position on the reef than ever. The crew could do nothing; it was useless to try to haul the heavy 150-ton schooner off the reef with her own boat and the canoes. Yet for the second time that month the Raroia reef was balked of its prey.

About noon the same day the schooner *Tamara* came in sight on the horizon to westward. She had been sent to fetch us from Raroia, and those on board were not a little astonished when they saw, instead of a raft, the two masts of a large schooner lying and rolling helplessly on the reef.

On board the *Tamara* was the French administrator of the Tuamotu and Tubuai groups, M. Frédéric Ahnne, whom the governor had sent with the vessel from Tahiti to meet us. There were also a French movie photographer and a French telegrapher on board, but the captain and crew were Polynesian. M. Ahnne himself had been born in Tahiti of French parents and was a splendid seaman. He took over the command of the vessel with the consent of the Tahitian captain, who was delighted to be freed from the responsibility in those dangerous waters. While the *Tamara* was avoiding submerged reefs and eddies, stout

Towed by the government steamer *Tamara,*
the *Kon-Tiki* arrived in Papeete harbor.

hawsers were stretched between the two
schooners and M. Ahnne began his skillful and
dangerous operations, while the tide threatened to drag both vessels on to the same coral
bank.

At high tide the *Maoae* came off the reef,
and the *Tamara* towed her out into deep
water. But now water poured through the hull
of the *Maoae,* and she had to be hauled with
all speed on to the shallows in the lagoon. For
three days the *Maoae* lay off the village in a
sinking condition, with all pumps going day
and night. The best pearl divers among our
friends on the island went down with lead
plates and nails and stopped the worst leaks,
so that the *Maoae* could be escorted by the
Tamara to the dockyard in Tahiti with her
pumps working.

TAHITI

When the *Maoae* was ready to be escorted, M. Ahnne maneuvered the *Tamara*
between the coral shallows in the lagoon and
across to Kon-Tiki Island. The raft was taken
in tow, and then he set his course back to the
opening with the *Kon-Tiki* in tow and the
Maoae so close behind that the crew could
be taken off if the leaks got the upper hand
out at sea.

Our farewell to Raroia was more than sad.
Everyone who could walk or crawl was down
on the jetty, playing and singing our favorite

tunes as the ship's boat took us out to the
Tamara. There was not a dry eye among them.

Those faithful souls who stood on the jetty
singing were losing six friends. We who stood
mute at the rail of the *Tamara* till the jetty
was hidden by the palms and the palms sank
into the sea were losing 127. We still heard the
strange music with our inner ear:

"—and share memories with us so that we
can always be together, even when you go
away to a far land. Good day."

Four days later Tahiti rose out of the sea.
Not like a string of pearls with palm tufts. But
as wild jagged blue mountains flung skyward,
with wisps of cloud like wreaths round the
peaks.

As we gradually approached, the blue
mountains showed green slopes. Green upon
green, the lush vegetation of the south rolled
down over rust-red hills and cliffs, till it
plunged down into deep ravines and valleys
running out toward the sea. When the coast
came near, we saw slender palms standing close
packed up all the valleys and all along the coast
behind a golden beach. Tahiti was built by old
volcanoes. They were dead now and the coral
polyps had slung their protecting reef about
the island so that the sea could not erode it
away.

Early one morning we headed through an
opening in the reef into the harbor of Papeete.
Before us lay church spires and red roofs half
hidden by the foliage of giant trees and palm
tops. Papeete was the capital of Tahiti, the
only town in French Oceania. It was a city of
pleasure, the seat of government, and the center of all traffic in the eastern Pacific.

One of the first to greet us was an old friend,
Chief Teriieroo.

When we came into the harbor, the population of Tahiti stood waiting, packed tight like a gaily colored living wall. News spreads like the wind in Tahiti, and the *pae-pae* which had come from America was something everyone wanted to see.

The *Kon-Tiki* was given the place of honor alongside the shore promenade, the mayor of Papeete welcomed us, and a little Polynesian girl presented us with an enormous wheel of Tahitian wild flowers on behalf of the Polynesian Society. Then young girls came forward and hung sweet-smelling white wreaths of flowers round our necks as a welcome to Tahiti, the pearl of the South Seas.

There was one particular face I was looking for in the multitude, that of my old adoptive father in Tahiti, the chief Teriieroo, head of the seventeen native chiefs on the island. He was not missing. Big and bulky, and as bright and alive as in the old days, he emerged from the crowd calling, "Terai Mateata!" and beaming all over his broad face. He had become an old man, but he was the same impressive chieftainly figure.

"You come late," he said smiling, "but you come with good news. Your *pae-pae* has in truth brought blue sky (*terai mateata*) to Tahiti, for now we know where our fathers came from."

There was a reception at the governor's palace and a party at the town hall, and invitations poured in from every corner of the hospitable island.

As in former days, a great feast was given by the chief Teriieroo at his house in the Papeno Valley which I knew so well, and, as Raroia was not Tahiti, there was a new ceremony at which Tahitian names were given those who had none before.

Those were carefree days under sun and drifting clouds. We bathed in the lagoon, climbed in the mountains, and danced the hula on the grass under the palms. The days passed and became weeks. It seemed as if the weeks would become months before a ship came which could take us home to the duties that awaited us.

Then came a message from Norway saying that Lars Christensen had ordered the 4,000-

The *Kon-Tiki* began its long voyage home on the deck of the steamer *Thor I.*

Good-by to Tahiti! Six wreaths floating shoreward were our promise to return someday.

tonner *Thor 1* to proceed from Samoa to Tahiti to pick up the expedition and take it to America.

Early one morning the big Norwegian steamer glided into Papeete harbor, and the *Kon-Tiki* was towed out by a French naval craft to the side of her large compatriot, which swung out a huge iron arm and lifted her small kinsman up on to her deck. Loud blasts of the ship's siren echoed over the palm-clad island. Brown and white people thronged the quay of Papeete and poured on board with farewell gifts and wreaths of flowers. We stood at the rail stretching out our necks like giraffes to get our chins free from the ever-growing load of flowers.

SIX WREATHS

"If you wish to come back to Tahiti," Chief Teriieroo cried as the whistle sounded over the island for the last time, "you must throw a wreath out into the lagoon when the boat goes!"

The ropes were cast off, the engines roared, and the propeller whipped the water green as we slid sideways away from the quay.

Soon the red roofs disappeared behind the palms, and the palms were swallowed up in the blue of the mountains which sank like shadows into the Pacific.

Waves were breaking out on the blue sea. We could no longer reach down to them. White trade-wind clouds drifted across the blue sky. We were no longer traveling their way. We were defying Nature now. We were going back to the twentieth century which lay so far, far away.

But the six of us on deck, standing beside our nine dear balsa logs, were grateful to be all alive. And in the lagoon at Tahiti six wreaths lay alone, washing in and out, in and out, with the wavelets on the beach.

Index

The Kon-Tiki Expedition covered
4300 nautical miles or a distance
equal to that from Chicago to Moscow

HAWAII

EQUATOR

South Equatorial Curr
(warm)

POLYNESIA

MARQUESAS IS.

FATU HIVA

SAMOA IS.

Sighted Puka Puka
July 30

Towed to
Tahiti

FIJI IS.

×

P

August 7,
Ran aground on

TAHITI Papeete

TUA

A

COOK IS.

RAROTONGA

Radio "ham"

RAIVAVAE

POLYNESIA

AUSTRALIA

NEW
ZEALAND

Map of the Kon-Tiki Expedition

COPYRIGHT BY
RAND McNALLY & COMPANY
MADE IN U.S.A.

NORTH AMERICA

PANAMA

GALAPAGOS IS.

ECUADOR
Quito
Guayaquil

Balsa logs cut here at Quevedo.
Floated down Palenque and
Guayas to Guayaquil

Logs taken by steamer
to Callao

PERU

June 10
Nearest Equator

Reported
site of reef

May 24

Humboldt Current

July 3

4300 NAUTICAL MILES IN 101 DAYS.
AVERAGE SPEED 42½ MILES PER DAY

(cold)

Lima
Callao

START
April 28

KON-TIKI
built here

Lake Titicaca

Tiahuanaco

SOUTH

REVA

PITCAIRN I.

EASTER I.

AMERICA

N

SWEET POTATO (kumara)

STONE STATUES OF SIMILAR CONSTRUCTION

STONE PYRAMIDS OF SIMILAR CONSTRUCTION